Creative IQ™

Giving Young Learners the Creative Edge in a Competitive World

Jo-Anne Schneeweiss

Shelley Sefton

Chestnut Publishing Group
Toronto

Copyright © Jo-Anne Schneeweiss and Shelley Sefton 2012

Library and Archives Canada Cataloguing in Publication

Schneeweiss, Jo-Anne, 1971 –
Sefton, Shelley, 1973 –

Creative IQ : giving young learners the creative edge in a competitive world /
Jo-Anne Schneeweiss, Shelley Sefton

Includes index
ISBN 978-1-926987-03-3

1. Activity programs in education.   2. Creative activities and seat work.   3. Creative ability in children.   4. Problem solving in children.   5. Social skills in children.   Title.

LB1027.25.S36 2012   371.3   C2011-907892-9

- Edited by James W. Black
- Photography by Ricki Horowitz
- Cover and design by Jim Muir
- Typesetting by Jim Muir

Printed and bound in Canada

Published by Chestnut Publishing Group
4005 Bayview Ave., Ste 610, Toronto, ON M2M 3Z9 Canada
Tel.: 416-224-5824   Fax: 416-486-4752

www.chestnutpublishing.com

We acknowledge the financial support of the Government of Canada through the Book Publishing Industry Development Program (BPIDP) for our publishing activities.

I dedicate this book to
my husband Reid and our daughters Rachel and Yael,
who inspire me every day.
Jo-Anne Schneeweiss

I dedicate this book to
my husband Daniel and my favourite assistant chefs,
Sabrina, Max and Dalia, who are learning the importance
of exploring their world in new and creative ways.
Shelley Sefton

Acknowledgements

Thank you to Stanley Starkman, the President and CEO of Chestnut Publishing Group, who believed in the concept of Creative IQ™ and took a chance to help us share our manuscript with you.

Thank you to Jim Black, our editor, whose experience, enthusiasm, and editorial insights were a constant source of guidance and support.

Thank you to Ricki Horowitz, our talented photographer, whose creative eye helped bring Creative IQ™ to life through images. You can view more of Ricki Horowitz's photography at www.rickihorowitz.com.

Thank you to Jim Muir, our design and layout director, who took great care to ensure that the final creative design of the book remained true to our vision.

Thank you to all of the children who participated in the Creative IQ™ photographs for your enthusiasm and patience:

Anita, Benjamin, Dalia, Eden, Isabelle, Matthew, Max, Quinn, Rachel, Sabrina and Yael.

Shelley: Thank you to my mother, a brave and courageous woman who taught me about the importance of inner-strength and following my dreams, and the benefits to being creative. I miss her every day. I also thank my father, a big fan of my culinary creations and a constant source of encouragement in all of my endeavours.

Jo-Anne: Thank you to my mother and father for their constant love and encouragement. They have always been present to talk, listen and dream in bright colours with me. I also thank my parents for showing me through their example that we all have an ability to make a positive impact in the world through our actions.

We are very grateful for our friendship, which was strengthened through the development, writing and publishing of Creative IQ™. We met through our oldest daughters who became friends on the playground at their new school. We subsequently discovered that our late grandmothers had been friends in South Africa, thus establishing a relationship that would span four generations of creative sharing and caring.

Contents

Introduction

We have always believed in the importance of teaching children to express themselves creatively. As teachers of art, drama, music, and cooking, we have seen the benefits of providing children with alternative forms of engagement and expression. As mothers, we have enjoyed watching our children experience the same enrichment from creative activities in our respective homes. Together we have identified and defined the term Creative IQ™ as an important part of a child's development, and collaborated in writing *Creative IQ™ – Giving Young Learners the Creative Edge in a Competitive World*.

Creative IQ™ - The ability to confidently develop and express creative, out-of-the-box solutions to challenges, relating to every aspect of life.

Our innovative book, *Creative IQ™ – Giving Young Learners Child the Creative Edge in a Competitive World*, embodies our combined teaching experiences, providing ideas for you as parents, teachers and caregivers to bolster a child's Creative IQ™ in a fun-filled, learning environment.

The book gives you fresh tools to teach young learners about a range of subjects, through different creative processes in your home or classroom. As you explore together the suggested activities organized by themes, engaged children will experience many different ways of learning and sharing information.

Developing a child's *Creative IQ™* is not meant to replace their academic learning, but rather to enhance it.

The Benefits of Creative Enrichment

Numerous benefits are achieved through early development of a child's *Creative IQ™* in an increasingly competitive world. Children with the ability *to think, process information, and express themselves creatively* will have an extra set of skills to draw upon as broad-minded, motivated adults, confident in their ability to make a valuable contribution to any group or endeavour.

1) **Creative Problem Solving** Children with a higher *Creative IQ™* will recognize that there are a number of ways to solve any given problem; consequently, they will be more likely to brainstorm alternative solutions and make effective choices.

2) **Visualization** A creative child will be able to visualize a multitude of possibilities beyond the obvious and beyond their physical environment. Visualizing success is a precursor to real success.

3) **Independent Thinking** A child's ability to offer their own suggestions when dealing with any given task will increase their comfort level in taking risks and relying on and/or offering their own ideas. Confidence and a sense of efficacy is the starting-point of personal achievement.

4) **Achieving Distinctive Project Results** A child, who can approach assignments creatively, will have the ability to achieve unique results both alone and in a group.

5) **Relaying Material in an Engaging Manner** The ability of a child to express himself or herself creatively will enhance their ability to confidently engage their audience verbally and visually.

6) **Relating to Different Types of People** An understanding of different forms of expression can enable a child to appreciate and relate to a variety of personalities and ideas.

Achieving Creative Enrichment

Each chapter or unit in *Creative IQ™ – Giving Young Learners the Creative Edge in a Competitive World* offers a broad spectrum of creative enrichment relevant to a different theme and Creative IQ™ Goal. The topics have been carefully chosen to pique children's interest and to stimulate their active participation.

Enrichment is gained through suggested art, music, drama, creative movement, cooking, science, mathematics and fitness activities. In fact, below each activity you will find the *building blocks for creativity* involved in the task, concepts that are subsequently defined in the book's glossary.

Several challenges have been included in each unit to extend activities for older children, and to make this a resource that can grow with your family or class.

Jo-Anne Schneeweiss & Shelley Sefton

Glossary

1. Creative Problem Solving

Analytical Skills Ability to analyze ideas, theories and problems through critical thinking.

Brainstorming Skills Ability to come up with ideas to solve problems.

Categorization Skills Ability to group objects and ideas into meaningful categories.

Comparison Skills Ability to compare objects, ideas and results.

Hypothesis Testing Skills Ability to formulate and test theories.

Investigative Skills Ability to conduct research, analysis and interviews.

List Making Skills Ability to make effective lists.

Memory Skills Ability to store and retrieve pertinent information.

Observation Skills Ability to store and interpret visual stimuli and information in the environment, and to record scientific findings.

Puzzle Solving Skills Ability to solve logical and mathematical problems.

Recording Skills Ability to capture data and create records.

Research Skills Ability to search for knowledge through resources such as books, magazines and the Internet.

Sensory Skills Ability to utilize the five senses (sight, hearing, taste, smell and touch).

2. Visualization

Art Appreciation Skills Ability to form opinions and judgments about art.

Artistic Skills Development of artistic expression.

Design Skills Ability to create artwork, an object or plan.

Innovative Thinking Skills Ability to think and plan creatively.

Life Skills Abilities including, but not limited to, kitchen skills, physical fitness skills, science skills, survival skills, risk-taking skills, nutrition skills

Marketing Skills Ability to create plans for promoting a product or service, and to communicate with a target market.

Musical Appreciation Skills Ability to form opinions and sensibilities about music.

3. Independent Thinking

Planning Skills Ability to create goals and objectives.

Decision Making Skills Ability to choose between different courses of action.

Reading Skills Aimed at improving reading skills.

4. Achieving Original Results

Implementation Skills Ability to plan and execute an idea.

Creative Writing Skills Ability to write fiction and non-fiction.

5. Communication Skills

Improvisation Skills Ability to act and communicate spontaneously.

Interpersonal Skills Ability to interact with other people and to respond appropriately in social situations.

Interviewing Skills Ability to ask effective questions to obtain the desired information.

Presentation Skills Ability to communicate ideas to an audience.

Verbal Skills Ability to express ideas clearly.

6. Relating to Different People and Different Ideas

Language Skills Ability to use appropriate grammar and vocabulary and to appreciate different languages.

Listening Skills Ability to be an effective and attentive listener.

Understanding of Cultural Diversity Openness toward and ability to learn about different cultures and societies.

Chocolotta...
Hard to Resist

We were excited to do the research and brainstorming for a chapter that required us to taste, smell and dream of chocolate. What could be more inspiring for children than activities involving eating, talking about and cooking with chocolate? Enjoy a real 'treat' together with your class or child.

Creative IQ Goal

The primary focus of this chapter is to develop a child's ability to examine an *area of commerce*, in this case chocolate. The activities are aimed at teaching children to use their five senses in order to consider or evaluate a product, to share what they have learned, and to market the product.

1) Treasured Chocolate

Children love to go on scavenger hunts and to solve clues as they search for hidden 'treasure,' in this case chocolate. Shhh…we won't tell if you don't!

Advance Preparation Create a series of clues for your home or classroom that will lead children to a chocolate treasure. Hold on to the first clue to give to the children at the beginning of the hunt, and hide the remaining ones, ensuring that the clues lead the young detectives to the chosen spots through to the final treasure. Examples are provided below for a home and classroom setting, which you can use, or you can create your own clues (although rhyming is not required).

At Home:

1. When you're dirty you want to laugh,
   But your parents say, it's time to … (bath)

2. It's late, and you need to rest your head,
   Where do you go? Why it's time for … (bed)

3. Nursery rhyme: The cow jumped over the moon,
   The dish ran away with the … (spoon – cutlery drawer)

In the Classroom:

1. Story time, where do you look
   When you want to find a … (book shelf)

2. If you want some time to play
   The crayons must be put … (crayon bin)

3. There's time to sing, and time to talk,
   And time to draw on boards with … (chalk container)

Announce the scavenger hunt and let the searching begin!

Challenge You supply the chocolate treasure and let the children create the clues and hiding spots for their own scavenger hunt to be solved by you or others.

Building Blocks for Creativity
- Investigative Skills
- Analytical Skills

2) I am Sweet

All children are special. It is important for each child to appreciate his or her various strengths in order to develop their confidence.

How do we do this and have fun at the same time?

Just like chocolate is made from a recipe, each child can now create a recipe describing himself or herself.

Step 1 Brainstorming

Ask your child to brainstorm or think of the qualities she likes best about herself before she begins to write down the ingredients in her own self-descriptive recipe. You may wish to share 'example ingredients words' such as helpful, kind and athletic, artistic, problem solver, and great giggler.

Step 2 Writing

Ask each child to write out an All About Me Recipe based on the qualities she chose to describe herself, or make one up together. You can show the recipe card example below.

Recipe Example Adina

Ingredients:

1 fast runner	1 great eater
1 puzzle solver	10 hugs
1 funny joke teller	10 kisses

Challenge ONE Have each child make up a recipe for each member of their family and encourage them to read the recipes aloud at the dinner table.

Challenge TWO Ask the learners to expand upon why each ingredient was included. For example:

I included "a funny joke teller" because I like to share jokes with my friends and family and make them laugh. I sometimes visit websites or look in books to find the best jokes to tell. Now that I'm older, I also make up my own jokes.

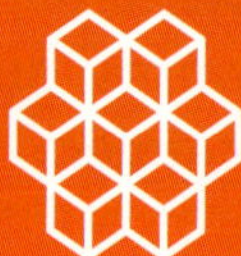

Building Blocks for Creativity
- Creative Writing Skills
- Brainstorming Skills

3) Sweet Chocolate Words

When the word *chocolate* is mentioned, it automatically inspires a series of sweet images for many people. The next activity involves a closer examination of this delicious 9-letter word.

Simply write *CHOCOLATE* on a piece of paper or chalk board and see how many smaller words your child or class can make using the letters, without using any letter twice. Some examples of smaller words found in "chocolate" include hole, tale, eat, cool and chat.

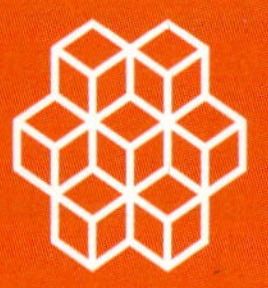

Building Blocks for Creativity
- Puzzle Solving Skills
- Language Skills

4) Chocolate Word Search

The word search below identifies the *main ingredients* found in chocolate, as well as flavourings and added ingredients.

Explain to children that a main ingredient takes a big part in creating the chocolate itself, such as cocoa beans, sugar and cocoa butter. A *flavouring* changes the flavour of the chocolate, such as mint, vanilla or coffee. Finally, an *added ingredient* is combined with the chocolate once the ingredients are mixed to add variety to the basic recipe and change the texture, such as crisped rice, nuts and fruit.

Now offer the word search below to discover chocolate ingredients.

Chocolate Word Search

Words

almond
caramel
cherry
cocoa beans
coffee
cream
crisped rice
fruit
milk
mint
nougat
orange
peanut butter
strawberry
sugar
toffee
vanilla

C	Q	R	B	C	H	E	R	R	Y	E	P
O	S	T	R	A	W	B	E	R	R	Y	E
C	B	R	Z	R	V	A	N	I	L	L	A
O	H	U	M	A	C	R	E	A	M	Y	N
A	V	F	O	M	I	L	K	R	Q	M	U
B	A	F	R	E	B	C	F	R	U	I	T
E	L	L	A	L	M	Y	O	G	E	N	B
A	M	E	N	R	P	C	E	F	O	T	U
N	O	U	G	A	T	Y	R	Q	F	D	T
S	N	B	E	X	T	O	F	F	E	E	T
L	D	Q	W	F	S	U	G	A	R	W	E
C	R	I	S	P	E	D	R	I	C	E	R

Challenge ONE

Have your children classify and record each search word as: (i) a main ingredient (ii) flavouring or (iii) added ingredient, as they solve the word search.

Answers:

Main Ingredients Milk, Cocoa Beans, Cream, Sugar

Flavourings Vanilla, Mint, Coffee, Orange (Cream), Strawberry (Cream)

Added Ingredients Peanut Butter, Cherry, Almond, Fruit, Caramel, Crisped Rice, Toffee, Nougat

Challenge TWO

Help children learn to carefully examine labels. Compare the ingredients listed on a chocolate bar wrapper or the sample label below to the search words listed above, and determine how many of them are the same.

Sample Label:

Ingredients Sugar, Milk Ingredients, Cocoa Butter, Cocoa, Lactose, Sugar, Wheat Flour, Modified Corn Starch

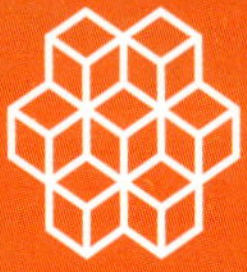

Building Blocks for Creativity

• Puzzle Solving Skills
• Categorization Skills
• Comparison Skills

5) **Chocolate** Sculpting

Q: What looks, smells and tastes like chocolate, but isn't chocolate?

A: Chocolate scented play dough (and we have the recipe for you below).

Chocolate scented play dough offers young learners the chance to develop their kitchen and fine motor skills and to have lots of sensory fun. The recipe provided below offers the chance to make a 'batch' together with your child or class. Then the young creators can either: (1) Design a sculpture on paper and then sculpt it with the dough, or (2) Create a sculpture right away.

Note: You may wish to save some of the play dough for activity #10 or make another batch.

Chocolate Scented Dough Recipe

You will need:

1¼ cups all-purpose flour

½ cup salt

½ cup cocoa powder

½ Tbsp lemon juice or white vinegar

1½ Tbsp canola oil

1 cup boiling water

Steps:

1. In a medium-sized bowl, mix together the flour, salt and cocoa.
2. Add the lemon juice, oil and water and mix quickly with a spoon.
3. When it has cooled, use your hands to continue mixing.

Note When you are finished with the chocolate play dough, do not forget to store it in an airtight container so that it does not dry out.

Challenge ONE

Ask children to shape the chocolate play dough to look like a cupcake or a brownie, and then press some real sprinkles on top. Let their peers or family guess whether it is real or not.

Challenge TWO

Introduce your child to two of the world's famous sculptors; examine together sculptures by Italian sculptor Michelangelo di Lodovico Buonarroti Simoni, otherwise known as Michelangelo (1475 to 1564) and French sculptor Auguste Rodin (1840 to 1917), online at a computer or on a smart board.

Many of Rodin's sculptures can be seen at the Rodin Museum in Paris, France (see: www.musee-rodin.fr or www.rodinmuseum.org), and Michaelangelo's famous David is at the Academia Gallery in Florence, Italy (see: www.uffizi.com/accademia-gallery-florence.asp).

You may stimulate discussion about the sculptures by asking the following questions:

i)   Have you seen any photos of these sculptures before?

ii) What kind of sculptures did each sculptor create?

iii) Did you notice anything unique or unusual about the sculptures?

iv) What types of material were used to create the sculptures?

v)   Which sculptures did you like best?

Then ask your child or students to use their chocolate play dough to create a model of one of the famous sculptures examined.

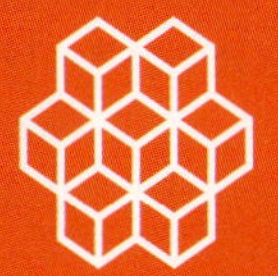

Building Blocks for Creativity

- Artistic Skills
- Art Appreciation
- Research Skills

6) Chocolate Capers

The next chocolate activity examines how well children know their chocolate bars, and requires them to use visual and analytical skills at the same time.

Advance preparation

Purchase up to ten popular brands of chocolate, which have not come into contact with nuts in their production (if allergies are a concern).

Then take the chocolate bars out of their wrappers and cut them into pieces so that their insides show. Place each brand on individual plates labelled from one to ten.

Eye on the Size

Ask your child or class to try to identify the chocolate brands on a piece of paper labelled from one to ten, using only their eyes to make a guess.

Note: You may choose to provide the names of the ten brands of chocolate used in the activity in advance of the guessing stage, thus facilitating the process for the children.

7) A Sweet Sensation

This next activity provides the opportunity for children to create an entirely new chocolate bar and to plan an advertising campaign to show it off to the world (or family).

Step 1 Brainstorming

Sit down together and *brainstorm*; consider the questions the learners need to answer about their chocolate bar before they begin designing the wrapper.

Points for discussion can include

a) What type of chocolate (milk, dark or white), intended flavourings and added ingredients do you plan to use?

b) Who will eat their chocolate? Children, adults or everyone?

c) What will be the shape of the chocolate bar?

d) What will be the name of the chocolate bar?

e) Will the chocolate bar have a nut-free certification (meaning it did not come into contact with any nuts in its production)?

Step 2 Designing the Wrapper

Children can use their favourite art supplies to design on paper a wrapper for their chocolate bar.

Step 3 Creating the Advertising Campaign

Now learners will have the chance to create a plan to spread the word about their chocolate bar, also known as an *advertising campaign*.

Time to be inspired! Ask the children to create one or more of the following advertisements as a way to spread the word about their new chocolate(s).

a) Posters

b) Newspaper or magazine advertisements (on paper)

c) Radio jingles (tape or video record their results)

d) Television commercials (video the commercial if you own a recorder)

Challenge Help children understand what "fair trade certified chocolate" means.

Over 200,000 children face abusive labour conditions picking cocoa beans in West Africa and many cocoa farmers are not paid enough to feed their families. Fair trade certified chocolate assures us that farmers received fair prices for their cocoa crops and that no abusive or unfair work practices were used at any stage of its production.

Discuss what your children could do to raise awareness about fair trade chocolate in their family or community.

a) Have each child create their own fair trade certified stamp design, in a form that will let them stick it on their new chocolate bar wrapper.

b) Consider having your child or classroom organize a Fair Trade Fair for their school.

Note You may wish to research Fair Trade Certified products yourself in order to provide children with a broader understanding.

Building Blocks for Creativity
• Innovative Thinking
• Marketing Skills

8) **Chocolate** Detective

Children use four of their five senses in this next delicious activity, as they play chocolate detective and try to guess what is inside ten different chocolate surprises (prepared by you). Sight, touch, smell, and taste are all required.

This activity also offers a great way to get kids to taste test foods they would be reluctant to otherwise try.

You will be covering an assortment of different food items with chocolate and asking your class or child to guess what is inside. They will then use a Detective Log (example provided below) to make note of the items used in the activity.

Advance Preparation

You will need:

10 small food items to cover with chocolate such as *pretzels, blueberries, strawberries, grapes, dried apricots, carrots, pepper slices, grape tomatoes, olives, marshmallows, cookies, brownies and chips*

8 ounces/250 grams of semi-sweet chocolate chips

canola or sunflower oil

parchment paper

Steps:

1. Cover a baking tray with parchment paper.
2. Melt the chocolate in a microwave or in a double boiler on the stove. Note: Watch carefully—chocolate can burn quickly.
3. Add a tablespoon of oil to the chocolate to thin it out for dipping.
4. Carefully dip each item into the melted chocolate and place on the parchment paper.
5. Once all of the food items have been covered in chocolate, place the baking tray in the refrigerator so that the chocolate will harden.
6. After the chocolate has hardened, place the items on parchment paper or plates, putting a number beside each item.

Note As a time saver, you may wish to visit your local grocery or bulk store, to see if you can find pre-prepared chocolate covered items.

Detective Work

Time to play chocolate detective as your child or class tries to identify the ten chocolate covered items on the tray!

Discuss the five senses and how *sight, smell, taste, touch* (and in other cases *hearing*) are important to *finding clues* and *to problem solving*. For example, ask children how they use their nose to decide what is in each chocolate shape.

Then let your child or students use their senses to try to identify each item on the parchment, recording their guesses in their Detective Log; depending on their age, you can record or discuss their guesses or have each child write them down.

Afterwards reveal the real food items.

A sample Detective Log is provided below, providing space for each child to record what their senses of telling them and to register their conclusion. For example, their senses might say soft, yellow, mushy and cold, and their corresponding conclusion, a chocolate covered banana.

Item #	What your senses say	Final Answer
1.		
2.		
3.		
4.		
5.		
6.		
7.		
8.		
9.		
10.		

Challenge

You can extend the activity to have each child write down their sight, smell, taste and touch descriptions for each item, as well as their conclusions.

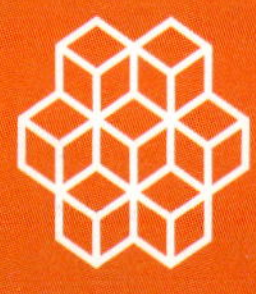

Building Blocks for Creativity

- Sensory Skills
- Investigative Skills
- Decision Making Skills

Treat Me

Baking is one of the best ways to experience the joy of chocolate. We are pleased to include a delicious Chocolate Baklava recipe for you to make with your child or class, or to share as a snack.

Chocolate Baklava

You will need:

1 package frozen phyllo dough, thawed

1¼ cups butter, melted

3 cups semi-sweet chocolate chips

2 tsp ground cinnamon

2 Tbsp cocoa

¾ cup brown sugar

Syrup:

½ cup apple or orange juice

½ cup sugar

½ cup water

½ cup honey

4 Tbsp lemon juice

Steps:

1. Preheat oven to 325 F.
2. Take 2 damp dish cloths and place the phyllo dough between them to prevent drying out.
3. Grease a 15-inch x 10-inch x 1-inch baking pan. Brush a sheet of phyllo dough with melted butter and place it in the pan. Repeat seven more times, adding each of the next seven sheets to the existing layers.
4. In a bowl, combine the chocolate chips, cinnamon, cocoa powder and brown sugar. Sprinkle 1/3 of the mixture over the top layer of phyllo dough.
5. Layer and brush four more sheets of dough with butter. Top with another 1/3 of the chocolate chip mixture.
6. Layer and brush four more sheets of phyllo dough with butter; top with remaining chocolate chip mixture. Top with the remaining phyllo dough, brushing each sheet with butter. Drizzle any remaining butter over the top.
7. Cut Baklava into 1½-inch diamonds using a sharp knife.
8. Bake at 325°F for 50-60 minutes or until golden brown.
9. Meanwhile, combine the syrup ingredients in a saucepan; bring to a boil over medium heat, stirring occasionally. Reduce heat to low; simmer, uncovered, for 20 minutes. Pour over warm Baklava.
10. Cool completely in pan on a wire rack.

Makes 16-18 servings

Challenge

Ask children to use the Internet or visit their school or local library to learn about Baklava's country of origin, as well as other foods eaten in that country.

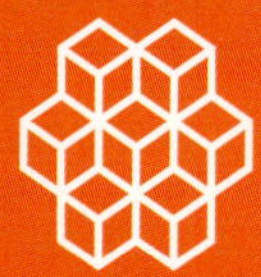

Building Blocks for Creativity

- Kitchen Skills
- Research Skills

   CHOCOLOTTA...Hard to Resist

10) Wrap it Up

Have children plan a chocolate party for their classroom, family or friends to launch their new chocolate bars created in activity #7 – *A Sweet Sensation*. Below is a '*to do*' list to assist the kids in their party planning.

To Do List for Children

1. Create and distribute invitations.
2. Sculpt an example of your 'chocolate bar' using chocolate scented dough.
3. Display your newly designed chocolate wrapper and any related advertisements for guests to see.
4. Bake treats for the party with your parent, teacher or caregiver – Chocolate Baklava!
5. Repeat some of your favourite chocolate activities from this chapter for guests to enjoy.
6. Decide how to introduce your new chocolate bar or bars, performing any jingles or commercials you created.
7. Discuss the importance of fair trade certified chocolate (if you completed the challenge in activity #7).

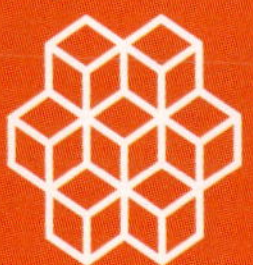

Building Blocks for Creativity

- Planning Skills
- Implementation Skills
- Presentation Skills

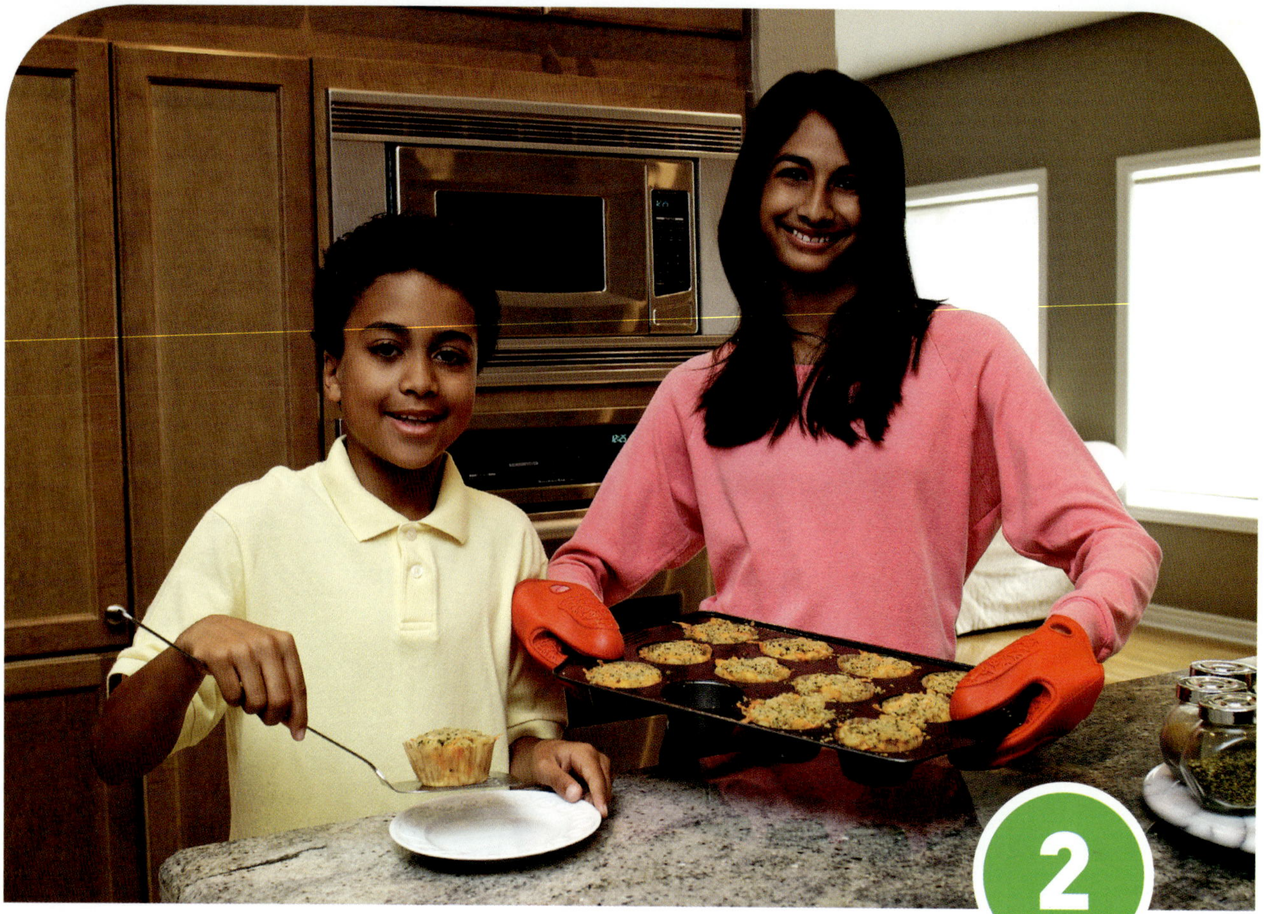

2

Creating in a
Winter Wonderland

Winter is a magical season – snow, holidays and sports have inspired songs, paintings, books, games and more for generations. Children can experience the wonder of the season indoors and outdoors with their family or classmates through the activities in this chapter.

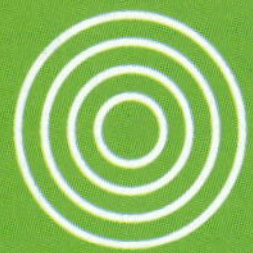

Creative IQ Goal

The activities set out below are designed to make children aware of the different seasons, and how we must adapt our behaviour in response to changes in the environment.

1) **Introducing** Meteorology

Meteorology is the scientific study of the atmosphere, with a focus on weather processes and forecasting.

In winter, weather forecasting is important because it helps people plan what to wear to stay warm, the amount of time to leave for a safe drive, whether there will be enough snow for winter sports, and more.

Experience this science in three different ways with children.

i) Make a list of different winter weather conditions and relevant forms of precipitation: e.g., ice pellets, snow storm, flurries, wind.

ii) Explain the function of adjectives as describing words to young learners and give them examples such as cold, freezing, slushy, chilly. Ask the children to make up a list of adjectives that describe winter weather.

iii) Let each child pretend that he or she is a television weather reporter. Ask him or her to use weather conditions and adjectives from their lists to present a weather report.

Weather Report Example

This is Jane Smith reporting for CAN News with your weather report for the weekend. Get out your snow shovels and warmest winter jackets because it is going to be cold.

On Saturday we are expecting seasonal temperatures of minus five degrees celsius. A winter storm is expected to arrive at 9 am and bring up to ten centimeters of snow. The snow should end at about 4 pm, leaving very icy road conditions. Police officers are warning drivers to plan for a slow drive and to take care on the roads.

Sunday will be clear and sunny, but still cold, with temperatures dropping to minus ten degrees celsius.

It's a great weekend to snuggle up with some books, bring out your board games, and build a snowman in the backyard.

Challenge

Let young learners continue building their storytelling skills. Ask each child to imagine he or she was the puck that won the Stanley Cup, and to describe their experience orally and/or in writing. Illustrations and sound effects can also be used to bring the story to life.

2) It's Freezing Cold

As just discussed, cold temperatures can make the water on the road freeze and become icy. Salt is often used to break up the ice and make the roads safe again. The science experiment set out below helps children appreciate the effect of adding salt to the melting process.

Experiment to Examine the Effect of Salt on Ice

You will need (per table of four to six students in a classroom setting):

2 plates

2 ice cubes

1 tablespoon of table salt

paper

pencil

Steps:

1. Place each ice cube on a plate.

2. Coat the top of one ice cube with 1 tablespoon of table salt.

3. Observe what happens to the ice cube with and without the table salt on top at intervals of five minutes.

4. Record your observations in writing or through drawings. You may wish to provide children with the science experiment worksheet provided in Appendix A for these purposes.

5. Consider the effect of salt on the speed of the melting process in writing up your conclusions.

Note Salt creates a chemical reaction that releases heat when added to ice, speeding up the melting process.

Let children consider the effect of salt on the ability of water to freeze, through the experiment below.

Experiment Examining the Effect of Salt on the Freezing Process

You will need:

two bowls of the same size

water

salt

Steps:

1. Label one bowl #1 and one #2.
2. Fill each bowl with I cup of water.
3. Add 2 Tbsp of salt to bowl #2 and stir it into the water.
4. Place both bowls in the freezer (or outside where the bowls will be visible, if the temperatures are below zero degrees celcius).
5. Examine both bowls every twenty minutes, and record how much the water has frozen in each bowl.
6. Write down your observations over a three-hour period.
7. Compare how long it took the water to freeze in each bowl.

Ask the children to research online or in the library why it takes longer for water containing salt to freeze.

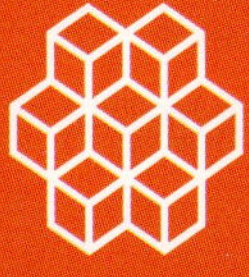

- Hypothesis Testing Skills
- Recording Skills

3) Igloo Sugar Cubes

An igloo is a kind of snow house, traditionally built in a dome shape by the Inuit people.

Find examples of igloos with young learners online and then let each child construct their own igloo using sugar cubes and icing. The objective is to create a design that will prevent the igloo from caving in.

Instructions for Making an Igloo out of Sugar Cubes

You will need:

cardboard	sugar cubes
pencil	vanilla icing
white paint	plastic knife
coconut flakes	paper plate

Steps:

1. Take a square piece of cardboard and draw a circle in the centre with a pencil (a pizza box can be used for this purpose). The circle should be between seven to eight inches in diameter.

2. Use white paint to cover the cardboard, except for the interior of the circle which should be left unpainted.

3. Sprinkle coconut flakes on the white paint while it is wet, ensuring again that there is nothing covering the area inside the circle drawn with pencil.

4. Start building your sugar cube igloo by laying out the first row of sugar cubes around the circumference of the circle you have drawn. Be sure to leave a space open for the entryway. The sugar cubes do not have to touch; they can be placed a little bit apart. At this point you are not gluing the cubes to the base.

5. Continue by creating a second layer of sugar cubes on top of the first. Use the white icing as the glue to keep the sugar cubes stuck together. Use a plastic knife to spread the icing over the cubes. Make sure that the sugar cubes of the second layer cover the spaces left in the first layer.

6. Using the sugar cubes and icing, make three to four more layers, placing enough icing to ensure that the sugar cubes are well stuck together. Put the structure aside to dry for an hour.

7. Place the structure on a paper plate. Create the next four layers by aiming slightly inwards towards the centre of the structure. Continue to use sufficient icing for the glue between the cubes.

8. Measure the top opening of the igloo and then cut out a circle-shaped piece of cardboard to cover it. Use the icing to glue the cardboard on the top opening on the top layer of cubes. Cover the cardboard with icing and then place enough sugar cubes over it, to cover. Allow to dry.

Tip If you do not have white icing, you can always use white school glue. It will do the job well, and looks just as good.

Note If you have the chance to play in real snow, ice cream scoops double as excellent snowball makers for children.

Challenge Research the natural environment that normally surrounds igloos. Then ask each child to draw a picture of their igloo, together with the surrounding environment.

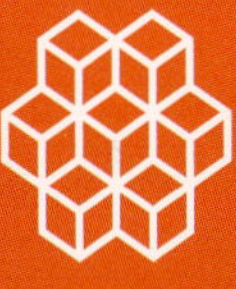

Building Blocks for Creativity

• Design Skills

4) I'm Wild About the Arctic

The cold weather conditions of the Arctic make it suitable for particular animals who can adapt to a very cold climate.

Let young learners uncover animals living in the Arctic, by unscrambling the letters to solve the Arctic Animal Jumbles below.

Arctic Animal Word Jumbles

1. **lowf**
2. **ssael**
3. **raolp rsbea**
4. **lrsauw**
5. **ruiabco**
6. **glbuea lehwa**
7. **niffup**
8. **neeerrin**
9. **rlahnwa**
10. **ynwso lwo**

Answers

1. wolf
2. seals
3. polar bears
4. walrus
5. caribou
6. beluga whale
7. puffin
8. reindeer
9. narwhal
10. snowy owl

Challenge
Have children research a list of additional animals that live in the Arctic, and have each child create their own jumble puzzles for friends and family.

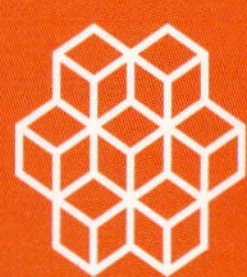

Building Blocks for Creativity
- Puzzle Solving Skills
- Research Skills

5) Snowflake...
You're truly unique!

No two snowflakes are exactly the same shape. This is due to the water molecules inside them that grow at different rates and in different patterns, depending on their exposure to humidity and temperature as they fall to the ground.

Young learners can make their own truly unique snowflake(s) out of paper.

Make Your Own Paper Snowflake

You will need:

a sheet of paper and a pair of scissors

Steps:

1. Take a piece of paper and cut it into a square shape.
2. Fold your square in half diagonally, so you have a triangle.
3. Fold your triangle in half – again, diagonally.
4. Fold the triangle shapes into thirds. If you fold one third to the back and one third to the front, it is easiest.
5. Take the shortest side of the triangle and cut a small arc out of it.
6. Cut some fun shapes or designs.
7. Finally unfold your paper and look at your creation.

Building Blocks for Creativity

• Artistic Skills

6) ComfOrt Food

We have included simple comfort food recipes below, aimed at warming you up on cold winter days. Enjoy making the recipes together with your child or class.

Pas'ta Macaroni Muffins Please

Macaroni Muffins – it gives a whole new meaning to the term "Mac & Cheese."

You will need:

½ cup seasoned bread crumbs

2 Tbsp olive oil

½ tsp salt

2 cups uncooked elbow macaroni (whole-wheat preferably)

1 Tbsp butter

1 egg, beaten

1 cup milk (1% or skim)

1½ cups shredded cheddar cheese

Steps:

1. Preheat oven to 350°F and grease a muffin pan with non-stick spray.
2. In a small bowl, stir together bread crumbs, olive oil and salt.
3. Bring a large pot of water to the boil, add the macaroni and cook for about 8-10 minutes.
4. Remove the pot from the heat, drain and return to the pot. Stir in the butter and egg until the pasta is evenly coated.
5. Stir in the milk and 1 cup of the shredded cheddar cheese (reserving the other ½ cup).
6. Spoon into the prepared Muffin pan. Sprinkle the reserved cheddar cheese and bread crumb mixture over the tops.
7. Bake for 30 minutes in the oven or until the tops are nicely browned.
8. Allow the muffins to cool a few minutes before removing from the pan.

Makes 12 muffins

Note These can be easily frozen.

Eggcellent Egg bread Souffle

You will need:

¾ cup butter

1¼ cups brown sugar

¼ cup maple syrup or corn syrup

1 large square egg bread, sliced

5 large eggs

¾ cup milk (1%, 2% or homogenized)

¾ cup light cream or half and half

1 Tbsp vanilla

½ tsp salt

Steps:

1. Spray a 9" by 13" casserole dish with non-stick spray.
2. In a saucepan, melt the butter, brown sugar and maple syrup.
3. Pour melted butter mixture into the bottom of the casserole dish.
4. Cut the sliced bread in half and remove the crusts.
5. Arrange the slices in one layer of the casserole dish, with slices slightly overlapping.
6. In a medium bowl, beat the eggs, milk, cream, vanilla and salt together.
7. Pour over the bread, cover and refrigerate for 8 hours or overnight.
8. Preheat oven to 350°F and bake uncovered for 40-45 minutes, until golden.

Serves 10-12 people

Note Serve warm, with maple syrup on the side.

7) What Kind of Key Makes Winter Fun? Hockey!

Winter festivals can be a great way to enjoy the best of the season together with your friends, family and neighbours.

Have each child examine the winter festival activities listed below, and choose which of them he or she would select for their festival. Young learners should feel free to add their own favourite winter activities. In a classroom setting, you may wish to complete this activity in groups.

ice skating	**hot chocolate**	**crafts**
snow shoeing	**fort building**	**hockey**
dog sled rides	**live entertainment**	**luge**
ice sculpting	**sledding**	**skiing**
face painting		

Challenge

Let each child (or group of students) choose a location near their school or home that could accommodate all of their chosen activities. Then have each child (or group) make a poster advertising their festival, drawing as many of their chosen activities as possible.

Building Blocks for Creativity

- Marketing Skills
- Planning Skills

8) snow Way I'll be Unprepared

Winter road conditions can leave cars stuck on ice or in snow. Children can help their families get prepared for winter by brainstorming what their parents should put in a survival kit for the car. Items can include anything from a favourite toy to a flashlight. Have each child prepare a list for you.

Note Here are some additional suggestions to consider for an Emergency Car Kit - car phone charger or a fully charged phone, emergency flares, first aid kit, flashlight, basic tools, jumper cables, blanket, sleeping bag, books or toys, mittens, snow hats, candy

Challenge

Ask children to put together a kit with their family to store in the trunk of the car for winter. In the case of a classroom, send additional instructions home to parents, together with their child's list from school.

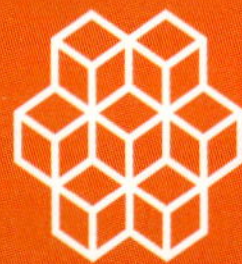

Building Blocks for Creativity

- Hypothesis Testing Skills
- Recording Skills

9) Cool **Hotel**

The Hotel de Glace or Ice hotel in Sainte-Catherine-de-la-Jacques-Cartier, Quebec, is redesigned and rebuilt each year out of snow and ice. The snow archways and ice sculptures provide a cool introduction to a one-of-a-kind winter holiday experience.

What would your students' or child's ice hotel design look like? Have each child design their own ice hotel on paper, including such things as a lobby, restaurant, rooms and so forth.

Photos and information about the Hotel de Glace can be found at: http://www.icehotel-canada.com (*at the time this book went to print*).

Challenge ONE

Have each child prepare a list of special steps or items which would be required to ensure guests' comfort at their ice hotel. Examples may include extra warm blankets, fireplaces, candles and lots of hot chocolate.

Challenge TWO

Let each child design a travel flyer or poster to encourage people to visit their ice hotel.

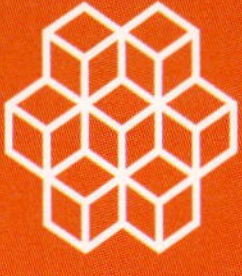

Building Blocks for Creativity

- Design Skills
- Brainstorming Skills

10) Hiber**nation** is a Sleepy Place

According to the *Concise Oxford English Dictionary (2012)*, the word hibernate is a verb; (an animal or plant) spends the winter in a dormant state.

Let children take a closer look at the word hibernation, by seeing how many words they can make out of the letters that make up the word.

Examples of words found in hibernation include nation, not, note, hear, bear, tire and hint.

Challenge Ask young learners to research the changes that happen in an animal's body when it hibernates and when it comes out of hibernation.

Questions for discussion:

1. What happens to an ainimal's body when it hibernates?
2. Is hibernation different from sleep? If so, how is it different?
3. Why do animals hibernate?
4. Give examples of types of animals that hibernate?

Building Blocks for Creativity • Brainstorming Skills

Math...
It All Adds Up

Math is not only something we learn in school. As children, and especially as adults, we encounter it all day long. From dividing up a box of crackers at snack time among a class of students, to following recipes, we are adding, subtracting and figuring out percentages every day, and all through this chapter.

Creative IQ Goal

These next ten activities are designed to demonstrate to children the many ways in which we use math every day, and how much fun it can be when everything adds up.

1) **Paint by** Number

Create a 'paint-by-numbers' activity to enjoy with your child or class.

Print a colouring page off of the computer, or create your own line drawing. Then number the different defined sections, and create a table indicating what colour each numbered section should be painted. In the case of a class, make copies for each student to complete.

Building Blocks for Creativity
• Comparison Skills

2) **The** Math **of Cooking**

When children grow up, they spend an increasing amount of time cooking and following recipes in the kitchen. This next activity examines and compares the different ways we can measure ingredients.

You will need:

measuring cup

measuring spoons

paper

writing utensils

Steps:

1. Divide the children into groups in a class setting.

2. Have young learners record how many tablespoons and teaspoons respectively there are in the following measurements of water by removing it slowly from the cup in each case:

   a) ¼ cup

   b) ⅓ cup

   c) ½ cup

   d) ⅔ cup

   e) ¾ cup

   f) 1 cup

3. Ask children to see how many teaspoons of water are in one tablespoon by measuring out a tablespoon of water into a bowl and then taking it out again with a teaspoon.

Note In order to help children develop the ability to form a hypothesis or prediction, you may ask each child to hypothesize how many tablespoons or teaspoons will be in the next measurement after he has completed steps 2 (a) and (b) in the activity above.

Challenge

If you have a scale available, measure out one (1) cup of various non-liquid ingredients in your kitchen or classroom, then weigh the same quantity, and have young learners record the results; e.g., rice, pasta, flour and icing sugar. They will see that one (1) cup of ingredients does not necessarily produce the same weight.

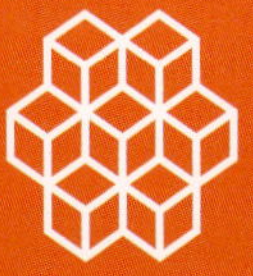

Building Blocks for Creativity

- Comparison Skills
- Science Skills

3) Unit to Measure it

Height is an important unit of measurement. It also provides a good chance for children to gain experience using a ruler or tape measure. You will need five stuffed animals for this next activity.

Tallest to Smallest Help young learners appreciate height differences by asking them to organize the stuffed animals from the tallest to the shortest.

You Take me to New Heights Present your child or groups of students, with a ruler or tape measure and help them measure the height of each stuffed animal. Have them record the results. Discuss whether the actual measurements matched their visual assessment above.

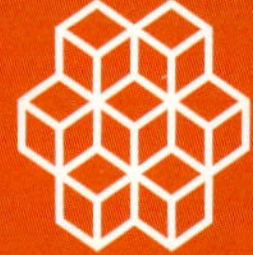

Building Blocks for Creativity
- Comparison Skills
- Recording Skills

4) You can Count on Me

Let young learners reflect upon the different ways we use math in our everyday lives by 'brainstorming' a list together. For instance, deciding on the amount of time needed to walk to a birthday party, and measuring out the amount of medicine required in one dose when sick.

Challenge An older child will be challenged if asked to write out their list within a set amount of time, i.e., five minutes.

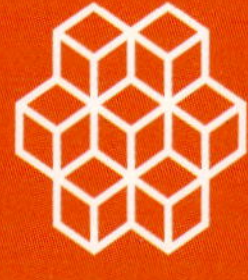

Building Blocks for Creativity
- Brainstorming Skills
- Verbal Skills

5) Patterning
a Friendship Bracelet

Patterning is also an important math skill. Your child or class can create their own unique pattern as they make a friendship bracelet out of Fruit Loops, Lifesavers or a variety of dry pastas. Have each learner design a pattern on paper first using the colours available, and then string on the 'food beads' to complete her creation.

Note This activity can also be completed with real beads if available.

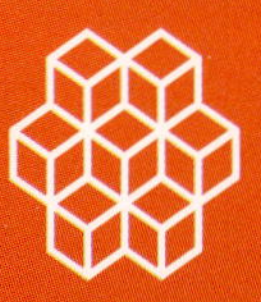

Building Blocks for Creativity
• Design Skills

6) Order Anything You Want in my Restaurant

Young learners can enjoy role playing and experience math in action, by creating their own pretend restaurant.

This exercise will involve making their own menu, including menu items with prices, setting a table, waiting on customers (that may be you!), and then adding up the bill to figure out the total amount owed, to develop writing, spelling and math skills. It will also encourage pretend play.

To Do List for Kids Creating Their Own Restaurant

- Decide on a name for the restaurant, and the hours it will be open.

- Create a menu for the restaurant, including breakfast, lunch and dinner items, along with their prices.

- Make order sheets with the name of the restaurant, leaving space on the sheet for the server's name and the table number, and space to write down the customer's order.

- Make checks or bills listing the items ordered, quantities, price, and the total amount owing on the bill.

- Design restroom signs for men, women, family and handicapped.

- Create open and closed signs for the door.

- Make kids colouring page and crayons if it is a family restaurant.

- Set the tables with place mats, napkins and eating utensils.

Note

- You can cut out pictures of food from magazines, use plastic food or you can use play dough to create the food.

- For money you can use Monopoly money or use dried beans or pasta for currency.

- Consider creating a "today's special" board for a special finishing touch.

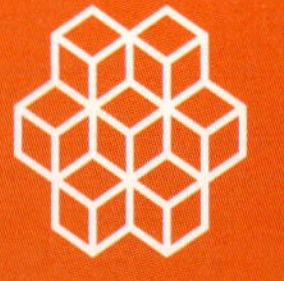

Building Blocks for Creativity
- Improvisation Skills
- Planning Skills
- Implementation Skills

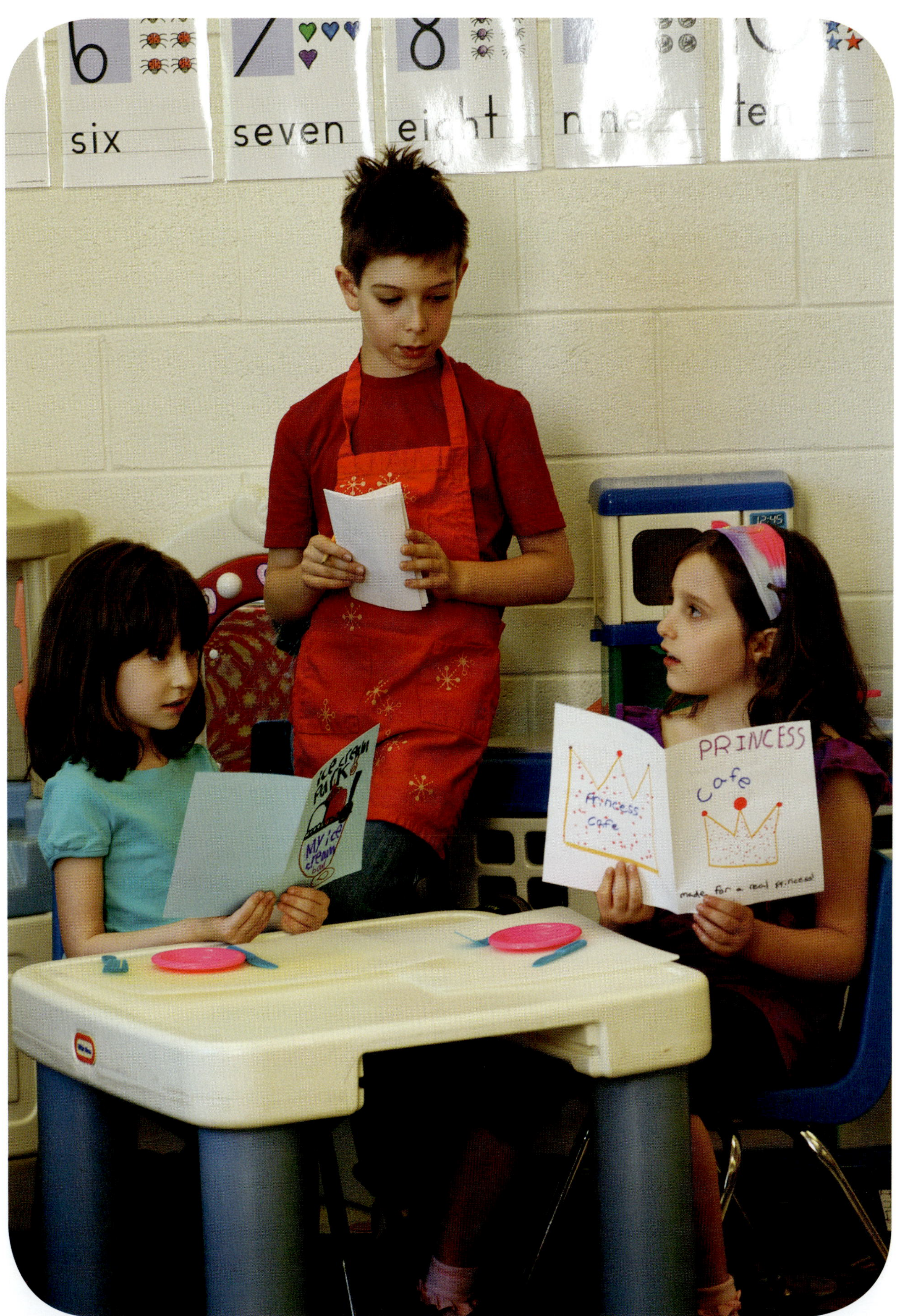

six
seven
eight
nine
ten
ICE CREAM PARLOR
MY ICE CREAM
PRINCESS
cafe
Princess
cafe
made for a real princess!

Count **Us In**

Recreational games can help children learn basic math skills. You can find two examples to enjoy together with your child below in *What Time is it Mr. Wolf?* and *Hopscotch*.

Instructions for *What Time is it Mr Wolf?*

1. The children line up along a wall.

2. At the other end of the room is Mr. Wolf.

3. In unison, all of children yell "What time is it, Mr. Wolf?"

4. Mr. Wolf, with her back turned to the children, yells out a time like "8 o'clock!"

5. The children take 8 steps towards the leader.

6. After two or three turns of calling out times, the children will yell "What time is it Mr. Wolf?"

7. The "Wolf" will yell "Dinner time!," turn around and run after the kids.

8. The children must run back to the wall they came from before they are caught.

9. Whomever the "Wolf" catches becomes the new wolf.

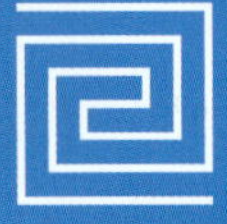

Challenge

Using a big piece of paper or chalk on a driveway or schoolyard, let children create hopscotch games, writing the numbers one to ten in each of the different shapes, and then let them try out their new playing course(s) together.

How to Play Hopscotch

1. Player one tosses his rock or pebble into the first square. The rock must land completely within the square without touching a line or bouncing out. If the rock lands in the wrong square, the player's turn is over. Otherwise, the player hops through the hopscotch court beginning on square one.

2. Side by side squares are straddled, with the left foot landing in the left square, and the right foot landing in the right square.

3. Single squares must be hopped on one foot.

4. Squares labelled "Safe," "Home" or "Rest" may be hopped through in any manner.

5. When a player reaches the end of the court, he turns around and hops back through the court, moving through the squares in reverse order and stopping to pick up his rock on the way back.

6. Upon successfully completing the sequence, the player continues his turn by tossing his rock into square number two, and repeating the pattern.

7. If while hopping through the court in either direction, the player steps on a line, misses a square, or loses his balance, his turn ends. The next player starts on her next turn where the player last left off.

8. How to win: The first player to complete every numbered square on the hopscotch court wins the game.

Building Blocks for Creativity

• Physical Fitness & Leisure Skills

8) Multiply **the Fun**

We are pleased to offer a tasty example of mathematics below.

Kids love to guess how many candies are in a jar. Absorbed with all the fun, they don't even realize that the game also involves estimating, counting and volume!

Fill a jar with gummy spiders and have your child or class guess the number of spiders. Then have them take out the spiders and count how many spiders are actually inside.

Note If gummy spiders are not available, simply use your favourite treat or snack food.

Challenge ONE

If you do use gummy spiders, you can also explore addition, subtraction and multiplication with your child, as you examine the number of spider legs on one and more spiders; i.e., two spiders have 8 + 8 legs or 8 X 2 legs, or 16 legs.

Challenge TWO

You can also teach your child about fractions using food. Place a pizza, pita, sandwich, fruit or pile of pretzels (or food of your choice) on a plate. Examine how to divide the food into quarters, in half and into thirds together.

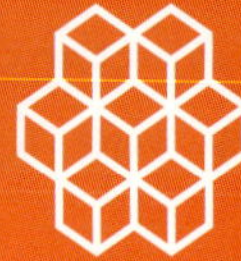

Building Blocks for Creativity

• Analytical Skills

9) Math Shapes Our Lives

Enjoy a variation of the popular *I Spy* game played in the Colour Chapter with your child or students (found in chapter 5, activity 9) to help develop shape recognition. Instead of having each child guess something you see of a special colour (i.e., *I Spy* With My Little Eye something that is red), ask each child to guess something you see that matches a specific shape; i.e., *I Spy* with my little eye, something that is round. Reverse roles to give your child the chance to identify shapes first, or let students find a partner and enjoy the game in pairs.

Challenge ONE

Another Dimension Play *I-Spy* using 3-dimensional shapes which have length, width and depth (e.g., a cube, prism or pyramid).

Challenge TWO

Far Out! Let your child independently create their own 3-dimensional shapes by connecting mini-marshmallows together with toothpicks.

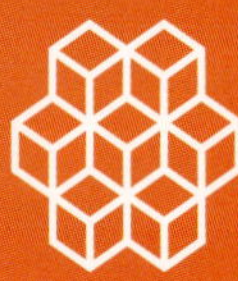

Building Blocks for Creativity

• Kitchen Skills
• Innovative Thinking Skills

10) Feed Your Mind

Now that your students or child have practiced different kitchen measurements, they are ready to apply their kitchen math skills, by preparing the recipes below.

Kitchen Sink Cookies Kitchen sink cookies get their name from the large number of different ingredients included. You should measure them out together with your young learners, to help them practice their measurement' skills.

Kitchen Sink Cookies

You will need:

1 cup unsalted butter, softened

$\frac{2}{3}$ cup firmly packed light-brown sugar

$\frac{1}{3}$ cup sugar

2 large eggs

1 tsp vanilla extract

1½ cups all-purpose flour

½ cup whole wheat flour

1 tsp baking soda

½ tsp baking powder

½ tsp salt

2 cups old-fashioned rolled oats

2 cups chocolate chips (semi-sweet, white, milk or a combination)

1 cup chopped pecans or walnuts

1 cup sweetened flaked coconut

1 cup dried cranberries or raisins

1. Preheat oven to 350°F. Spray baking sheets with non-stick spray or use parchment paper.

2. In a food processor fitted with a steel blade, beat butter and white and brown sugars for about 2 minutes.

3. Beat in eggs one at a time and then vanilla, until well blended.

4. In another bowl, sift together flour, white and wheat flours, baking soda, baking powder and salt. Gradually add butter to the mixture until well blended.

5. Add oats, chocolate chips, pecans, coconut and cranberries and pulse 10-15 times, until mostly mixed.

6. Drop batter by heaping tablespoons onto baking tray. Press tops down with the back of a fork to flatten.

7. Bake for 16 to 18 minutes. Cool on pan and then remove.

Makes about 48 cookies

Recipe Wizardry Let your young learners create their own fruit salad recipe. Present individuals or groups with pre-cut fruits and let them select their own quantities of ingredients, place them in a bowl, and record all recipe ingredients on paper.

Challenge Ask older children to *compare* the number of one fruit used versus another, also known as a *ratio*. For example, eight banana slices were used, and sixteen grape halves, at a *ratio* of one banana slice for every two grape halves.

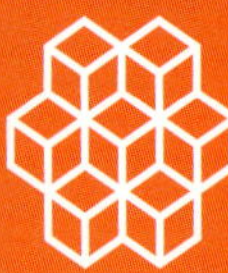

Building Blocks for Creativity

- Kitchen Skills
- Innovative Thinking Skills

Little Chili Peppers...
A Journey to Mexico

There are many ways that you can creatively teach children about a country and its culture in the comfort of your home or classroom. Now is a great time to grab your imaginary sombrero, suntan lotion and beach towel, and get ready to visit the 14th largest country in the world.

Creative IQ Goal

The primary focus of this chapter is to develop a child's ability to relate to different people and ideas, by strengthening their appreciation of cultural diversity.

1) Flag **it down**

Flags offer a sense of pride, history and, national identity to countries. They fly at important national landmarks and schools, as well as at international institutions and sporting events. Each flag, of course, is characterized by its own individual colours and design.

Recognizing Mexico's flag will let children know that they have arrived in the country or that Mexico has a presence at an international event or group.

Share and explain the significance to the country of the images on the Mexican flag, pictured and described below.

There are three vertical bands in green, white and red.

Mexico's national coat of arms appears in the white centre of the flag. It reflects the ancient Aztec legend that their capital city was to be settled where they saw an eagle eating a serpent while sitting on a prickly pear cactus (which they named Tenochtitlan, now known as Mexico City). The national colours appear in the ribbon at the base of the coat of arms.

Compare the elements of the legend with the flag itself.

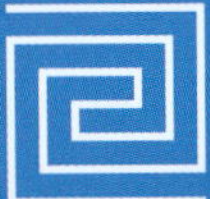

Challenge

Discuss with your class or child the significance of the colours, symbols and history of your own country's flag. You may wish to research in advance the flag's background or read together a relevant book on the subject. Then ask the children to copy and colour their country's flag on a separate piece of paper. They can then attach a straw or stick to their paper to create their own waving flag.

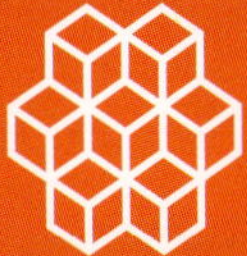

Building Blocks for Creativity

- Observation Skills
- Comparison Skills
- Artistic Skills

2) Move & Groove

A country's music offers an opportunity to experience their language and culture in a new and different way.

Put on a Spanish music CD from the library or a store, and dance together with your child or students. Dancing is a great form of exercise, and the music will introduce children to the distinctive melodies of the Spanish language.

Challenge

Examine the lyrics of the music with your child or class, and choose some random words or verses to translate with a Spanish-English dictionary.

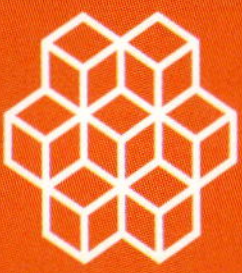

Building Blocks for Creativity

- Language Skills
- Physical Fitness Skills

3) Shake **it baby!**

Favourite musical instruments often differ between countries – those used to accompany the music that is enjoyed locally.

Maracas or shakers are percussion instruments often heard in Mexican music and played at festivals. They are filled with seeds or dried beans and played in pairs.

Now your child or students can design their very own Maracas and then learn about and practice making rhythms.

Step 1 Create 'One of a Kind' Maracas

You will need (to make two maracas):

4 paper plates with rims

writing utensils (crayons, pencil crayons, markers, etc.)

white school glue

beans, rice or seeds

1. Have the children decorate the base of four paper plates with writing utensils to design the exterior of the maracas.

2. Ask the children to place two of the plates coloured side down. Pour approximately ⅓ cup of beans, rice or seeds onto the middle of each of the two plates.

3. Glue the rim of each paper plate to the rim of one of the two remaining paper plates. Press the rims together and wait for the glue to dry (waiting is the hardest part of the whole activity).

Note You can staple the two paper plates together for each child, if you do not have enough time to wait for the glue to dry.

Explain the meaning of a *pair*, in this case of maracas, to younger children.

Step 2 Create 'Sound Pictures' with Rhythm

The definition of a *Musical Rhythm* can be simplified for children as follows:

Rhythm is like the drawings you make, except with sound. You know you have made a particular drawing because of the way that colours and shapes *are organized* on a page. Every picture is different. Rhythm is like a 'sound' picture, identified by the way *'what you hear' is organized* – how the sounds are made, such as loud or quiet (*volume*), soft or short (*accent*), the speed or the pace of the sounds (*tempo*) and the way in which they are arranged (*meter*).

Demonstrate for the children an active example of a rhythm or 'sound picture' with a maraca. Describe the way in which 'what they hear' is organized.

You make a rhythm with one of the maracas for the children. Have them repeat it with their own maracas. Reverse roles and let the children create rhythms for you to play back.

In a classroom, you may ask the children to divide into pairs and repeat this exercise with each other.

Challenge ONE Help your child or class understand the *elements of music*, by singing or playing recordings of their favourite songs, and then have them try to repeat the rhythm with their maraca.

Note In a classroom, you may wish to divide the students into smaller groups and create a Music Festival of Bands to complete challenge two.

4) Piñata **Power**

Some of the activities or traditions your child or class enjoy in their lives may have been borrowed from other cultures. Piñatas offer a great example.

Piñatas originated in Mexico and are still often found at Mexican celebrations. Typically piñatas are made out of brightly coloured paper mache or cardboard containers, filled with candy, fruits or toys, and then suspended in the air. Blindfolded children try to break open the piñata with a stick in order to get to the treats.

Excitement with piñatas is now widespread, and they can be found globally at birthday parties involving children.

Bring the thrill associated with piñatas in your own home or classroom.

Let your child or students design their own piñata on paper, and then write or dictate a list of all the treats and toys they would place inside.

5) **On the** Ball

Many countries tend to favour specific sports. Mexicans are passionate about recreational and professional soccer on the local sports fields and in the country's major stadiums.

Your child or class can experience the excitement of the sport through the following activity.

Supplies required:

soccer ball or equivalent

pylons or substitute

Set-up a line of pylons approximately three (3) feet apart outdoors or in an open space indoors. Encourage each child to kick the ball around the pylons back and forth, concentrating on how their body is moving the ball along.

Then take away the ball, and have each child pretend to kick an imaginary ball the same way.

Building Blocks for Creativity
- Physical Fitness Skills
- Improvisation Skills

6) Count **on Me**

The desire and ability to interact with people from different countries and cultural backgrounds builds open-mindedness and connects communities.

Spanish is the most commonly spoken language in Mexico. Now you can give children the ability to communicate with the locals in Spanish (or at least a start), by teaching them the numbers from one to ten.

It's as easy as uno, dos, tres.

English	Spanish	Pronunciation in Spanish
zero	thero	cero
one	oo-no	uno
two	dos	dos
three	tres	tres
four	cuatro	kwat-ro
five	cinco	theen-ko
six	seis	seys
seven	siete	syet-ay
eight	ocho	o-cho
nine	nueve	nwe-bay
ten	diez	dyeth

Challenge Review with the children the additional commonly used Spanish vocabulary provided below.

Everyday words

hello	hola	o-la
goodbye	adios	a-dyos
how are you	como estas	como es-ta
please	por favour	por-fa-vor
thank you	gracias	grath-y-as
good	buenas	bwen-os
morning	dias	dee-as
bathroom	el bano.	ell-bon-yo
restaurant	restaurante	rest-au-ron-tay
good	buenas	bwen-os
night	noches	no-ches
yes	si	see
no	no	no

7) **That is** Puzzling**!**

Every country has its own characteristics that make it special.

The word search below is a fun puzzle and a journey into the sights, tastes and language of Mexico. Discuss the relevance of each word with your class or child and ask them to categorize whether it falls under sights, tastes or language. Then let your child or students have fun finding the words discussed, having gained a greater appreciation for their relevance.

Mexico Word Search

Words

adios
beans
burrito
chilli
como estas
gracius
guacamole
maracas
ola
quesadillas
salsa
sangria
sombrero
taco
tortilla

B	G	M	B	M	Z	B	Q	Y	S	X	W
Q	U	E	S	A	D	I	L	L	A	S	Q
Y	A	V	Q	R	X	M	B	V	L	Q	T
Y	C	X	B	A	B	E	A	N	S	M	O
B	A	T	A	C	O	Y	Z	B	A	G	R
Z	M	Q	M	A	X	B	X	U	V	R	T
B	O	Q	B	S	A	N	G	R	I	A	I
O	L	A	X	Q	D	L	P	R	Y	C	L
X	E	Z	C	H	I	L	L	I	M	I	L
M	B	Y	V	I	O	Z	B	T	V	A	A
C	O	M	O	E	S	T	A	S	S	S	S
N	S	O	M	B	R	E	R	O	B	Q	Z

8) Bean There, Done That

Los Frijoles or beans in Spanish, have been important to the Mexican diet for thousands of years. In fact, many of the different varieties and colours in the world today were first cultivated in Mexico.

Your child or class can appreciate the variety and colours of dried beans by using them as art materials to create mosaics, an artwork made up of different materials.

Mexican Bean Mosaics

Supplies required:

a variety of dried beans

cardboard, cardstock or other thick paper

glue

Steps:

1. Ask your child or students to decide on a picture or mosaic they wish to create on the paper using the beans.

2. Have the children create an outline for the picture with pencil on the cardboard.

3. Then ask him or her to glue different kinds and colours of beans between the lines to create their 'Mexican' Mosaic.

Note Extend this Mexican Mosaic activity by taking your class or child with you to choose from among the dried beans available at the store; examples include split green peas, split yellow peas, red lentils, black eyed peas and barley.

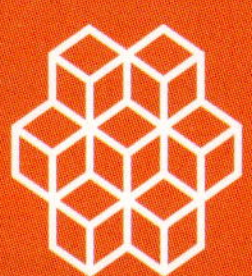

Building Blocks for Creativity • Design Skills

Sugar, Spice, and Everything **Nice**

In many cases, a country's food is identified with certain spices and dishes. It may be as a result of local food production or historical traditions. We experience their specialties in the country itself or in local restaurants featuring national cuisine.

Mexican cuisine includes many recipes with chilies, herbs, beans and tomatoes.

Introduce your students or child to the 'tastes of Mexico,' while teaching them kitchen skills, as you make *Quesadillas, Nachos* and *Mexican Hot Chocolate* together. Alternatively, you can make these recipes in advance and share it for a themed lunch or snack.

Quesadillas Recipe

You will need:

4 tortillas (whole wheat is preferable)

1 chicken breast, cooked and sliced

1 tomato, diced

1 cup Monterey Jack or cheddar cheese, shredded

1 onion, sliced (optional)

Steps:

1. Preheat oven to 350°F.
2. Place 2 tortillas on a baking sheet that has been sprayed with a non-stick spray.
3. Place chicken strips on the tortilla, top with tomatoes and then sprinkle with shredded cheese.
4. Top with the other two tortillas and bake in the oven for 8-10 minutes.
5. Carefully remove from the oven (you will need an adult to do this).
6. Cut into 4 triangles and serve.

Serves 2 people

Note Be sure to let the quesadilla cool before cutting it. Consider using a clean pair of scissors to cut it into quarters.

Microwave version The quesadilla can be put in the microwave for 30-45 minutes on high.

Vegetarian option Omit chicken and use grilled vegetables (coloured peppers, onions, zucchini and eggplant).

Nachos Recipe

This recipe makes a great snack and group activity – putting out the toppings in little bowls with spoons and letting the kids pick and choose to make their own.

You will need:

aluminum foil cut into large squares (approximately 11"x 11")

non-stick cooking spray

tortilla chips

cheddar cheese, shredded

salsa

light sour cream

green onions, sliced

olives

fresh tomatoes, diced

green chilies, chopped (optional)

Steps:

1. Preheat oven to 400°F.
2. Spray the foil with the non-stick spray.
3. Place a layer of chips at the bottom.
4. Top with a little of each of the toppings you like.
5. Sprinkle shredded cheese on top.
6. Fold the edges of the foil pouch up around the nachos.
7. Bake for 6-8 minutes, until the cheese is melted.
8. Carefully remove from the oven (you will need an adult for this).

Mexican Hot Chocolate

The word chocolate has its origin in Mexico where the Maya and Aztecs made it into a beverage they called xocolãtl. Today Mexican hot chocolate is distinguished by its hint of cinnamon.

Try the recipe below and encourage the children to do a taste test and compare it to their favourite version.

Ingredients:

3-4 Tbsp granulated sugar

3 Tbsp unsweetened cocoa

¼ tsp ground cinnamon or a cinnamon stick

2½ cups milk (1%, 2% or homogenized)

½-1 tsp vanilla extract

Steps:

1. In a small heavy-duty saucepan, combine the sugar, cocoa and cinnamon.

2. Over medium heat, gradually stir in milk until combined and hot, but do not boil.

3. Remove saucepan from heat and stir in vanilla.

4. Beat with a wire whisk until frothy and then pour into mugs or cups.

Makes 3 servings

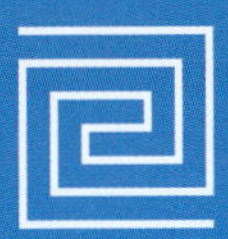

Challenge ONE

Smell different spices and extracts with your child or class and modify the recipe above to create a new hot chocolate drink together. Compare and contrast your results with those above.

Challenge TWO

Arrange a field trip to a local Mexican restaurant, and discuss their specialties and ingredients used with the owner or chef.

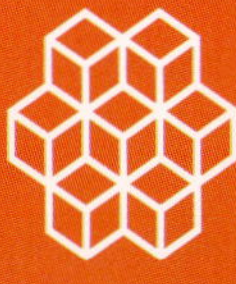

Building Blocks for Creativity

• Kitchen Skills

10) Fiesta **Time**

Combine all the above activities to create a Mexican Fiesta (or party) – real or imagined, for family, friends or another class.

A Kids' *'To Do List'* for their Mexican Fiesta

a) Make a guest list for the Fiesta.

b) Design your own invitations.

c) Hang up craft activities and puzzles.

d) Make a grocery list to prepare Mexican Food (Nachos, Quesadillas and Mexican Hot Chocolate).

e) Choose Spanish Music to play in the background.

f) Provide a soccer ball for guests to kick around.

g) Prepare the food.

h) Shake your maracas as guests arrive, and give them a turn.

i) Show off your Spanish whenever you need to refer to a number.

You Colour
My World

From an early age, we like to talk about our favourite colours. It is not surprising, since colours have such a strong effect on how we experience the world around us. We are delighted to help you add a splash of colour to enhance children's appreciation of the world around them.

Creative IQ Goal

This chapter is designed to make children more aware and appreciative of the impact of their colour choices when creating illustrations and presentations.

1) I see **Colours**

Red, Blue and Yellow are primary colours, or the colours from which all other colours are derived, except for black and white, which are shades. Children can enjoy the experience of creating new colours through their very own science experiment. Find the instructions below to help young learners create red, blue and yellow ice cubes, and then combine them together and let them melt, to see the new secondary colours that form – *orange* from red and yellow, *green* from blue and yellow, and purple from red and blue.

Ice Cube Colour Experiment

You will need:

3 ice cube trays

red, yellow and blue food colouring

re-sealable plastic bags or clear plastic cups

Steps:

1. Add a few drops of red food colouring to an ice tray. Carefully fill the ice tray with water and place in the freezer until frozen. Repeat these steps, using the yellow and blue food colouring in the other two ice trays respectively.

2. When the ice has frozen, place two red and two yellow ice cubes in a re-sealable plastic bag. As they melt, ask the children to observe what colour they create when the melted water mixes together. Repeat using red and blue, and blue and yellow combinations.

Note Before you throw out the bags of coloured water, consider the activity challenge below.

Challenge ONE Tertiary colours are made when secondary colours (e.g., green, orange and violet) are combined together with primary colours (red, blue and yellow).

"

Have the children create tertiary colours by mixing the secondary coloured water produced in the experiment above together with the following primary colour ice cubes in six separate sealable bags:

a) orange water + red ice cubes

b) orange water + yellow ice cubes

c) green water + yellow ice cubes

d) green water + blue ice cubes

e) violet + blue ice cubes

f) violet + red ice cubes

Ask each child to predict or hypothesize the new colour combinations that will result from the melting process, and then record their actual findings in words and pictures on paper.

Note There are six tertiary colours: Yellow-Orange, Orange-Red, Blue-Green, Yellow-Green, Red-Violet, Violet-Blue.

A visual guide to primary, secondary and tertiary colours can be found below to share with children and reinforce your findings.

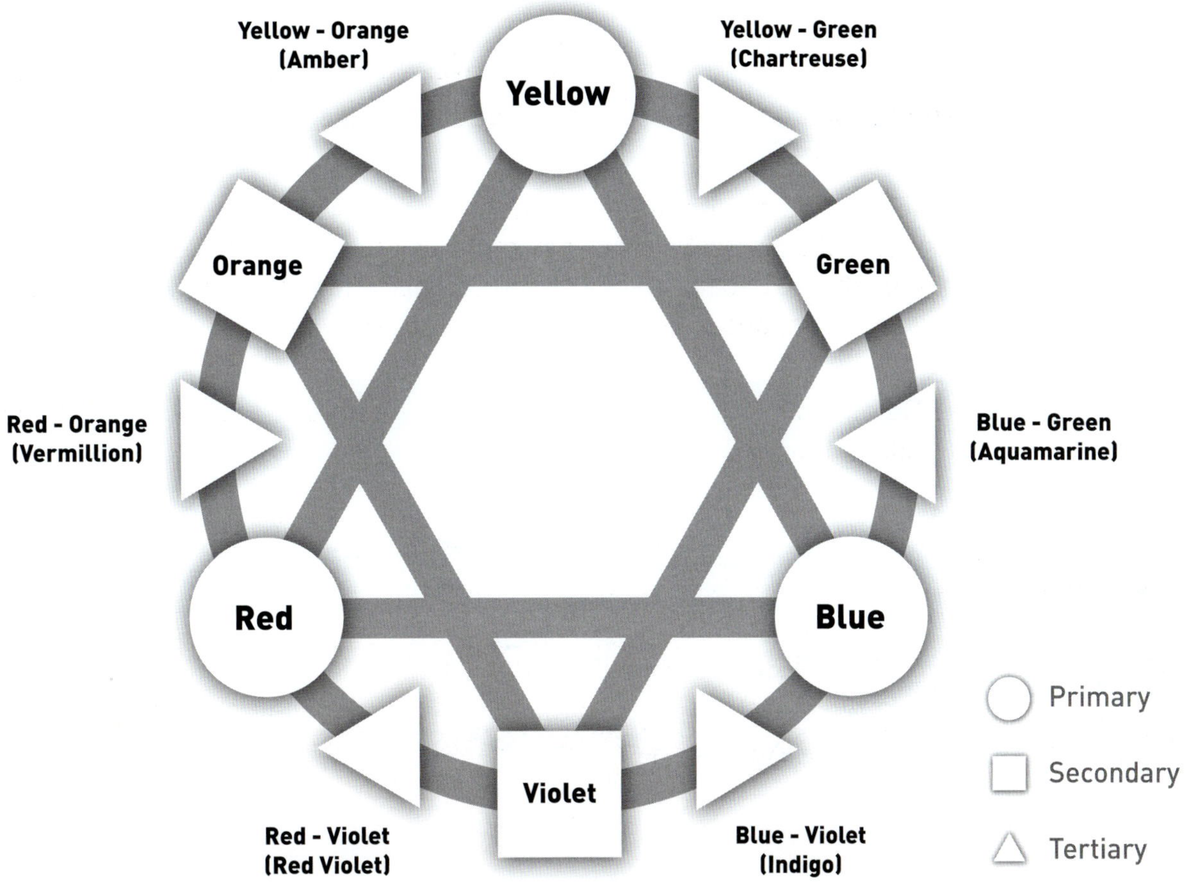

Challenge TWO

If you are in a season with snow outside, put the coloured water in spray bottles and let the children create snow art.

Note Make sure that the children are careful to keep the water away from their clothing as it may stain.

Building Blocks for Creativity

• Science Skills
• Categorization Skills

2) Where's Design for My Bedroom?

Give children the chance to develop drawing and decorating skills as they create their ultimate bedroom.

Have each child draw their ideal bedroom design with a pencil, black marker or crayon. Then photocopy the design several times so that young learners can use different colours to see which colour combination looks best.

Challenge

Ask the children to identify each of the colours used in their design as a primary, secondary or tertiary colour — thus helping to build on their classification skills learned earlier.

Building Blocks for Creativity

• Design Skills
• Categorization Skills

3) Pop Go The Colours

Andy Warhol is famous for his pop art. Among his vast collection of works are images which were reproduced, painted in bright colours and placed adjacent to each other creating bright, bold, colourful contrasts.

You can view some famous examples of Andy Warhol's pop-art style with young learners by searching for the following titles together on the Internet or in the library: "Campbell's Soup Can," "Ten Marilyns" of Marilyn Monroe, "Mickey Mouse," "16 Jackies," "The Beatles" and "Three Coca Cola Bottles."

Below are instructions for children to create their very own Andy Warhol pop-art style masterpiece.

Instructions to Create Andy Warhol Style Pop-Art

You will need:

8½ X 11 inch white paper

black pencil, crayon or marker

What to do:

At home

1. Have your child draw a picture on a piece of white paper with a black pencil, crayon or marker.

2. Photocopy the picture four times, and have him or her colour each replicated design in different colours.

3. Mount all of the pictures on a large piece of bristol board to achieve the full effect.

In a classroom setting

1. Divide students into groups of four.

2. Have each group work together to create one piece of artwork.

3. Take the artwork and photocopy it three more times.

4. Have each member of the group colour one copy of their artwork individually, without consulting with the other members of their group.

5. When they are done, bring the four pictures together and mount them on a large Bristol board to achieve the full effect.

Note You can add a framed effect to the artwork by mounting it on coloured bristol boards.

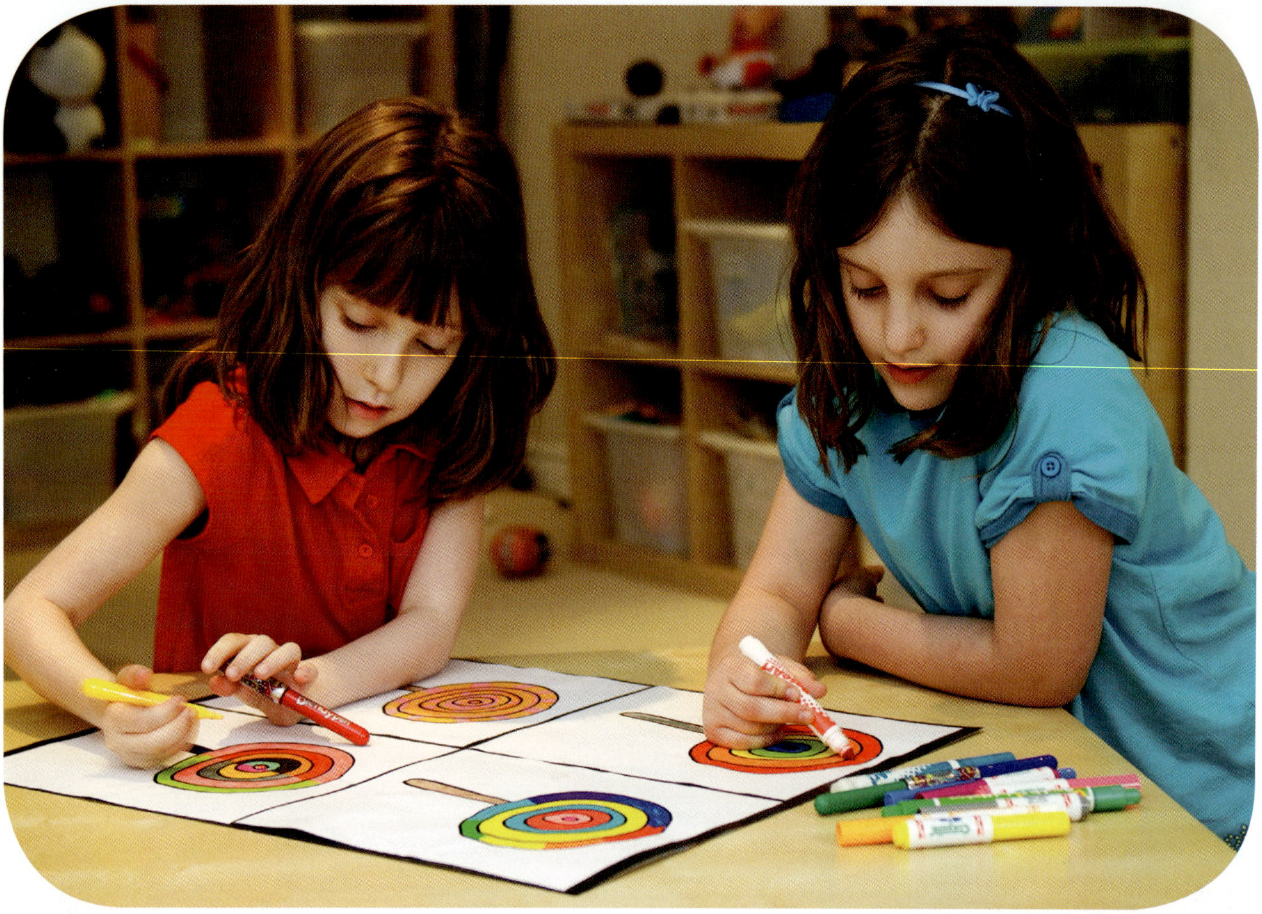

Building Blocks for Creativity

- Art Appreciation Skills
- Artistic Skills
- Research Skills
- Team Building

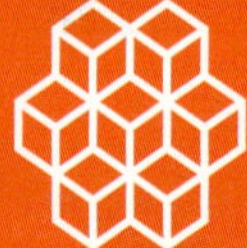

4) I'm Falling for You

In Fall, we admire the changing leaves as the deciduous trees transform into a display of brilliant colours.

Collect and preserve some coloured leaves this coming Fall to enjoy all-year-round.

Instructions for Drying Leaves

You will need:

a variety of leaves in different colours and shapes

a heavy book

several layers of waxed paper

Steps:

1. Place the leaves recently collected between clean sheets of wax paper.
2. Insert the wax paper containing the leaves between the pages of a heavy book.
3. Close the book and leave it on a shelf for several months.

When you open the book again, take the leaves out carefully. They can be used for home décor or art projects.

Challenge Ask children to research in books or online what causes the leaves to change colours during the Fall season.

Questions to Guide Research and Discussion

1. What changes in the environment let leaves know it's time to change colour?
2. What chemical disappears from the leaves when they change colour?
3. Which colours are left after the green chlorophyll leaves and why?

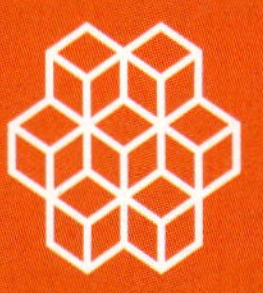

Building Blocks for Creativity
- Implementation Skills
- Research Skills

5) **Cooking with** Colour

The colour of food helps tell us if it is fresh, and can make it look either more or less tempting to eat. The recipes below will give children the chance to experience and taste multi-coloured ingredients, while building kitchen skills.

I've Bean Dreaming of Jelly Cookies

Jelly Cookie Recipe

You will need:

½ cup butter, softened

⅔ cup brown sugar, firmly packed

⅓ cup sugar

1 egg

1 tsp vanilla

½ tsp baking soda

½ tsp baking powder

½ tsp salt

1¼ cups all-purpose flour

½ cup rolled oats

1 cup jelly beans (you can use mini jelly beans or jelly beans cut into pieces)

Steps:

1. Preheat oven to 375°F and spray baking sheets with non-stick cooking spray.

2. Using a standard or hand-held mixer, cream the butter and sugars together. Add the egg and vanilla and mix.

3. Add the baking soda, baking powder, salt, flour and rolled oats. Mix until all ingredients are just combined.

4. Finally, stir in the jelly bean pieces.

5. Drop the cookie batter by spoonfuls onto the baking sheets (try to keep the mounds 2" apart).

6. Bake for 10 minutes. Remove from the oven. Allow to cool for five to ten minutes on the sheet, then transfer with a spatula to baking racks to cool completely.

Makes about 3 dozen cookies

Note Feel free to substitute Smarties or M&Ms for the jelly beans.

I'm truly Cookie for Stained Glass

Stained Glass Cookie Recipe

You will need:

½ cup butter

1 cup white sugar

1 egg

1¾ cups flour

1 tsp baking powder

1 Tbsp milk or water

½ tsp vanilla

20 coloured hard candies (unwrapped!)

re-sealable plastic bags

large and small shaped cookie cutters

non-stick spray

Steps:

1. Place butter, sugar and egg into mixer and mix until creamy.

2. Add flour, baking powder, milk and vanilla and continue to mix until smooth (you can add some extra flour if dough is too sticky or wet).

3. When dough is ready, place bowl in the refrigerator for twenty to thirty minutes, until it is firm.

4. Take hard candies and put into a re-sealable plastic bag. Use your rolling pin to crush the candies into small pieces.

5. Remove dough from the refrigerator and place on a well-floured surface.

6. Preheat the oven to 375°F and spray a baking sheet with non-stick spray.

7. Roll the dough out until it is flat and smooth. You may wish to sprinkle a little flour on the rolling pin before starting, to prevent the dough from sticking to it.

8. Take the larger cookie cutters and cut out a variety of shapes.

9. Take the smaller cookie cutters and cut out shapes in the centre of the large cookies you cut out before.

10. Carefully place the cookies on the baking sheet and fill the centres with the crushed coloured candies.

11. Bake cookies in the oven for eleven to fourteen minutes, until the edges are golden brown in colour.

12. When ready, remove from the oven. Allow to cool for five to ten minutes on the sheet, then transfer with a spatula to baking racks to cool completely.

- You can use any variety of clear candies. "Jolly Ranchers" or fruit flavoured "Lifesavers" are great options.

- You can place all of the candies in one re-sealable bag and crush them or you can use a different bag for each colour or flavour.

Challenge

Let children further strengthen their awareness of the relationship between food and colour. Choose and call out a colour. Then see how many foods each child can list in five minutes that include the colour chosen. Consider turning this brainstorming activity into a game, by participating yourself, or having children work individually to see who can come up with the longest list.

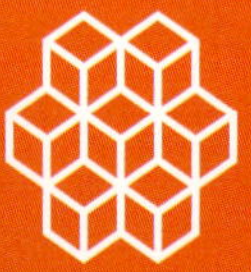

Building Blocks for Creativity

- Kitchen Skills
- Brainstorming Skills

6) **Tell Me Just One More** Colour

We experience colours with our ears as well as our eyes. When someone describes something, the listener sees a visual image with the colours described, and it appears in the person's mind or thoughts.

Young learners can enjoy a fun exercise that uses verbal and listening skills and emphasizes our mutual appreciation of colours.

At home

Choose a children's book with simple pictures. Then have either you or your child describe one of the pictures, including colour descriptions in words. The other person will draw what he hears being described using crayons, pencil crayons or markers. Afterwards, compare the drawing made with the picture in the book.

Repeat the activity, but switch roles.

At school

Divide the class into groups of two. Have one child in each pair choose a children's book with simple pictures. Then instruct the groups on the steps set out above for the home activity.

Challenge Have children see how many songs they can list, which include a colour in the lyrics; e.g., Baa Baa Black Sheep, Five Green and Speckled Frogs, Yellow Submarine. This exercise can be completed verbally or in writing.

Building Blocks for Creativity
- Verbal Skills
- Artistic Skills
- Brainstorming Skills

7) Roses are Red, Violets are Blue, I'm Writing the Poem You Asked Me To

Colours have inspired writers over the years. Now children will have the chance to write their own acrostic poem about their favourite colour.

In an acrostic poem, the title (topic) is printed vertically, letter by letter. Each letter is used to construct a phrase or sentence which describes the topic.

See an example of an acrostic poem about the colour red below.

Red is a primary colour.
Eating red berries is a healthy snack.
Drawing with red crayons is fun.

Now let each child create an acrostic poem about a favourite colour, or have them write one together.

You may wish to help young learners find inspiration for their poem through an informal discussion. Discuss the different reasons people like a colour.

Discussion Questions to Inspire Acrostic Colour Poetry

1. What is your favourite colour?

2. How did you pick your favourite colour?

3. Do you think of specific objects when you consider the colour(s)? If so, what are they?

4. Does the colour make you think of nature or something closer to home?

5. Does the colour make you feel a certain way when you see it?

Building Blocks for Creativity
- Creative Writing Skills
- Interpersonal Skills
- List Making Skills

8) Somewhere Over the Rainbow

Storytellers have long imagined a pot of gold guarded by leprechauns at the end of the rainbow.

A rainbow occurs when the light outside passes through the tiny drops of water in the atmosphere. The light is reflected through the water and comes out as a part of the color spectrum

A rainbow is an arc that shows all the colors, red, orange, yellow, green, blue, indigo and violet.

Rainbows can sometimes be spotted in the spray of lawn sprinklers, in the mist of waterfalls, and most spectacularly in the sky during a rain shower when the sun is still shining.

Ask children to use their imagination to decide what they might find at the end of a rainbow. Then have young learners act out an imagined trip to the end of the rainbow, individually or in groups, being sure to show what they discover.

Instructions for Preparing a Skit

a) Brainstorm a story to be acted out. Ensure that there is a beginning, middle and an end.

b) Assign roles to perform the story as a skit (if more than one person is involved).

c) Practice the skit, so that all persons involved know when they enter/exit the story. Further, children can determine if any props are required.

d) Make any props that are necessary to present the skit.

e) Perform and wait for the applause.

Remind children that it is as important to learn to be a responsive member of the audience as a performer. They must listen carefully.

Challenge Have each child write down their improvisation as a story or play script. He or she may choose to add illustrations as well.

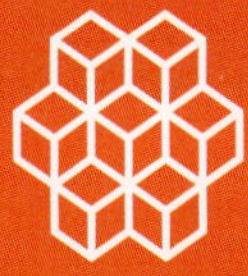

Building Blocks for Creativity
- Improvisation Skills
- Creative Writing Skills
- Artistic Skills

9) I Spy with My Brown, Blue or Green Eye…

I Spy is a great game for exploring the colours around you at any age. In fact, you probably remember it from your own childhood. In case you have forgotten the rules, we have included them below.

Instructions for Playing *I Spy*

How to play:

1. You will need at least two players.

2. The first player silently looks around to select an object that can be seen by all the players.

3. The player says "I spy with my little eye," and then gives some description of the object, such as "something red," "something blue" or "something pink."

4. The other player(s) take turns trying to guess what the object is.

5. Let the player who correctly guesses the selected item pick the next object, or have all players take turns in a set order (which may be best if you are playing with younger children who are not be so good at guessing).

6. Offer extra clues if the players are completely stumped.

Note This game does not work well on buses, or on car trips, because the objects outside go by too quickly.

Challenge ONE

Extend the activity to a second more active colour identification game when there is more than one child and a large open space is available. Instead of having the children guess the object spied in a room as above, have all the children run to any object that matches the colour verbally chosen by the leader; e.g., the leader will call out, "I see purple." The object of the game is for the children to find and get to any object matching the colour chosen as quickly as possible.

Questions for discussion may include:

1. Are you decorative?
2. Are you strong?
3. Are you harmful?
4. Where can I find you?
5. Would you rather be another colour? Why or why not?

10) I feel Blue

Colour has been connected with mood. It is accepted that different colours are supposed to influence our feelings one way or another. Both psychologists and interior designers have examined this phenomenon, in order to make people aware of the effects that colours in one's environment can have.

Have children conduct an experiment to examine if there is a pattern in the way specific colours make people in your classroom or home feel.

Instructions for Experiment Relating to Colour and Mood

What you need:

pencil
markers or crayons
piece of paper

1. On a piece of paper, draw circles and fill them in with some or all of the following colours: Red, Blue, Yellow, Green, Orange, Purple and Pink.

2. Write down the following eight feelings below the coloured circles on the same sheet of paper: happy, excited, sad, angry, scared, calm, comfortable and strong. Attach a number to each feeling listed on your paper.

3. Create a table on a separate sheet of paper to record the answers to the interviews you will conduct to gather the data or information for your experiment. Make a column for each of the colours being examined.

4. Interview individuals in your home or classroom. Show each person interviewed the coloured circles one at a time, and ask him or her to tell you which mood listed below each colour evokes in him or her. Record the number under the colour, and continue the interview with the other circles.

5. After all of your interviews are complete, record how many people associated each feeling or mood with a certain colour by adding up the results in each column.

6. Report on your conclusions in written form.

Challenge ONE

Invite a psychologist or interior designer to attend your classroom to speak with the children about colour and mood. Alternatively, contact a paint store, find out if there is a specialist available to discuss the effect of colour on mood, and organize a field trip to the store with your child or class. In either case, have the children present their own experiment findings to the expert(s) for their feedback.

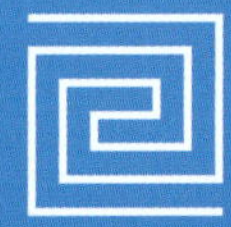

Challenge TWO

Ask young learners to research online or in books what psychologists and interior designers have said about the relationship between colour and mood, and compare the generally accepted findings with their own experiment's conclusions.

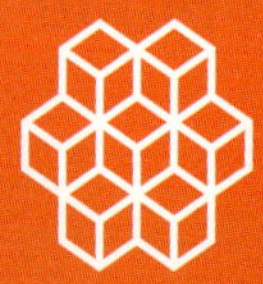

Building Blocks for Creativity

- Science Skills
- Interviewing Skills
- Comparison Skills

Surfing for Fun

at the Beach

The idea of a sandy beach is exciting for both children and adults alike. Of course, we are pleased to offer activities involving sand pails, shovels and other things to build your child's creative IQ.

Creative IQ Goal

In this chapter, seaside-themed activities are aimed at developing your child's ability to appreciate an experience, in this case an outing to the beach.

1) I Dream of Beaches

The ability to visualize all aspects of a project or experience is important to achieving effective results and planning at any age.

In this activity, children will create their *ideal, dream beach*.

Show the list of animals and activities below, all of which *may* be found at the beach, to your students or your child. Discuss any terms they may not know yet.

Then have them choose which ones they would like to have on their *dream beach* by circling the words. Ask your students or child if they would add anything to their ideal beach that is missing from the list.

Finally, ask young learners to draw their ideal beach referring to their lists.

Beach List:

umbrellas	seagulls
beach chairs	fish
beach pails & shovels	crabs
board walk	jellyfish
towels	sharks
sand	dune buggies
sandcastle building	para sailing
sea shells	boats
waves	surf and boogie boarding
rocks	beach volleyball
lifeguards	coral reef and scuba diving
ice cream	sunscreen

Challenge Have your class or child design a travel brochure or poster that would persuade people to visit their *dream beach*.

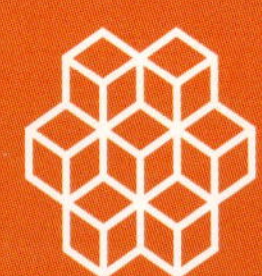

Building Blocks for Creativity
- Marketing Skills
- Artistic Skills
- Decision-making Skills

2) Shore, I like Volleyball

Recreation is an important part of a healthy lifestyle at any age.

Balloon volleyball can make beach volleyball an indoor or outdoor sport!

Explain to your class or child how volleyball works, using the rules below. Then let them practise basic volleyball skills with a balloon.

Basic Rules for Volleyball

You will need:

a balloon

a string or long piece of material to hang for the net

a scoreboard (optional)

The objective of the game is to use one's hands to hit a ball (or balloon) over the net so the opposing team is unable to hit it back.

The game is played by two teams that are divided by a tall net.

The game begins with one team serving the ball over the net to the opposing team. The two teams continue to pass the ball backward and forward over the net.

A team wins a volley when the receiving team hits the ball out of the defined court or lets it drop to the ground.

When the serving team wins a volley, it wins a point and the right to continue serving. The game is usually played until the first team has 21 points!

When the receiving team wins a volley, they do not gain a point, but the chance to serve; however, taking the age and skill level of the children into account, you may want to give the receiving team a point too when they win a volley.

Building Blocks for Creativity • Physical Fitness

3) How do You Like Your Float? With or Without Salt?

Below is a science experiment for young learners that examines whether adding salt to water, similar to what's found in the ocean, will effect whether an item floats or sinks in it.

Your class or child will be placing an egg in two glasses, one filled with fresh water, and one filled with salt water. They will then record their observations as to whether either egg floats or not.

Experiment Instructions

You will need:

two glasses

two eggs

tap water

kosher salt

measuring cup

Steps:

1. Take the two glasses, and fill each of them with tap water.

2. Add 6 tablespoons of Kosher salt to one glass of water, and stir it with a spoon. Leave ordinary tap water in the second glass.

3. Ask the children to hypothesize or predict whether the egg will float in each of the two glasses.

4. Carefully lower an egg into each of the two glasses with a spoon.

5. Discuss and record observations as to whether the egg floats or sinks in each of the two glasses.

What should have happened?

When salt is added to water and dissolves, it makes ordinary water denser. As a result, the egg should float in the salt water, and sink in the ordinary tap water.

Refer to Appendix A at the end of the book to see a sample form for recording the different elements of a science experiment, including the hypothesis, materials, method, observations and conclusion.

 **Challenge**

Have your child or class research the effects of the high salt content of the Dead Sea, bordered by Israel and Jordan.

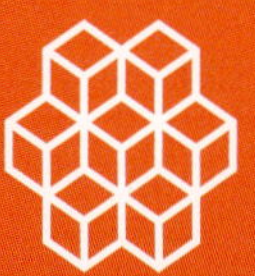 **Building Blocks for Creativity**

- Science Skills
- Hypothesis Testing

Leis **time at the Beach** but no Laziness

Leis, a wreath made of flowers, are given out in Hawaii as people arrive and leave the islands.

Below you will find instructions to help your students or child create a lei to put around their own necks or for their friends.

Instructions for Marking a Lei

You will need:

yarn or string

construction paper in a variety of colours

pencil

a pair of scissors

hole puncher

plastic drinking straws

Steps:

1. Cut the yarn into 20 to 25 inch pieces.
2. Take a pencil, draw flowers on the different coloured pieces of construction paper, and then cut them out.
3. Using a hole punch, make a hole in the centre of each flower.
4. Cut the drinking straws into 1 inch pieces, so they are ready to be threaded between each flower.
5. Thread the yarn through a flower and then a straw piece, alternating until the lei is the desired length.
6. Tie the ends of the lei together and you will have a brightly coloured, flower necklace.

You may wish to extend this activity by encouraging young learners to include a pattern within their lei by shape or colour.

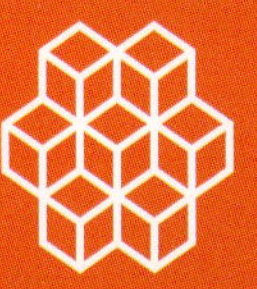

Building
Blocks for
Creativity
• Artistic Skills

5) Shark Encounter

Sharks fascinate people. Children or students can take a closer look at this fish by examining its anatomy together with you. Review the shark anatomy below.

During this *biology exercise*, children learn about the complexities of the body, and labelling, while developing their memory skills and an appreciation for science.

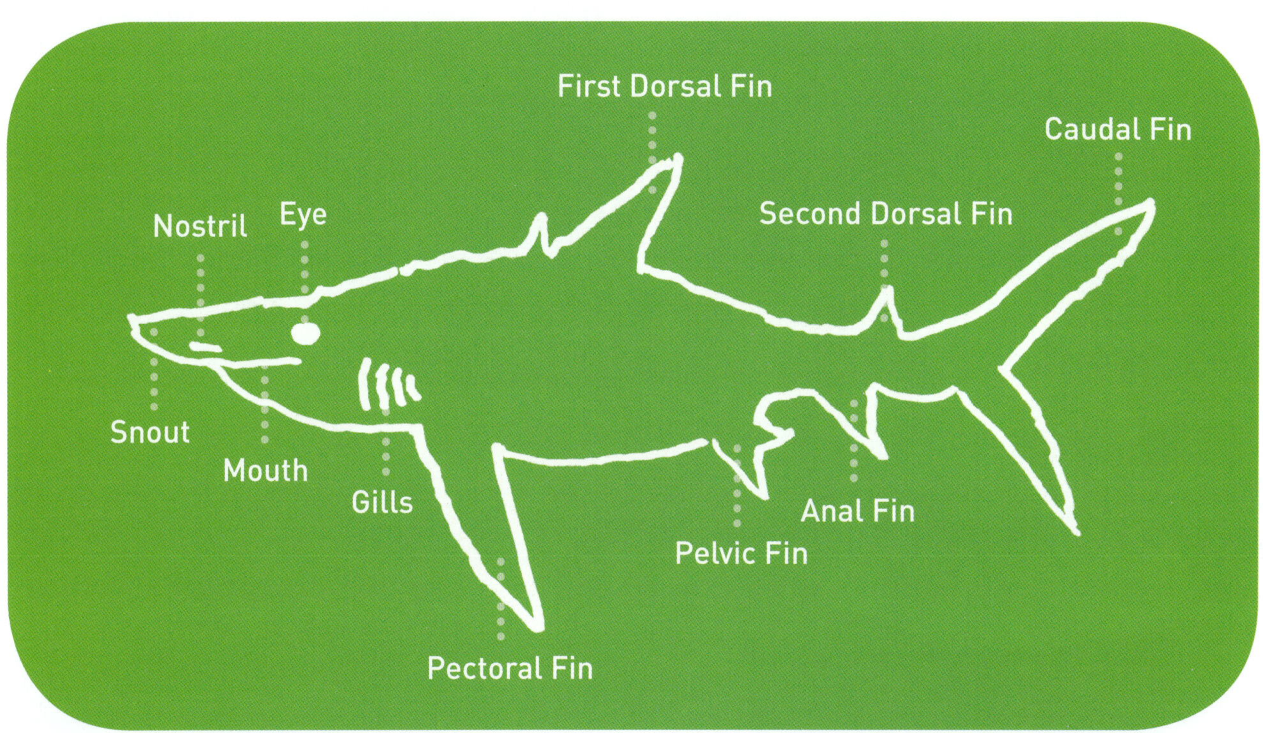

Challenge Visit the library or browse together the Internet to learn more about sharks.

Some questions to research and discuss may include:

a) What different kinds of sharks exist?

b) Where do sharks live in the world?

c) What do sharks eat?

d) From how far away can sharks smell blood?

e) What predators do sharks have?

f) Are sharks really a threat to humans?

6) This Sandcastle Puzzles Me

Sandcastle building is always a fun beach activity. The goal here is to create a spectacular design.

Through this activity, your students or child will be asked to visualize and build their own sandcastle 'puzzle' at home—and build it over and over again!

Have each child design a sandcastle on a piece of cardboard or cardstock. Then have him or her cut it out into puzzle shaped pieces for a sandcastle that can be re-built without making a mess.

Challenge

Improve your child's Internet skills, and share their amazement as you and they surf the web for professional sand sculpture displays.

Note *The Sandcastle Contest* written by Robert Munsch offers a fun look at creating realistic-looking sandcastles with silly results.

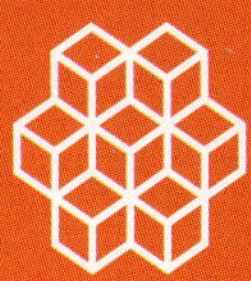

**Building
Blocks for
Creativity**

• Design Skills
• Research Skills

7) I'm going out on a Limbo

The Limbo Dance originated on the island nation of Trinidad in the Caribbean. It is a dance where participants move to the rhythm of the music while bending their bodies to fit underneath a bar.

Limbo is now widely enjoyed as a fun activity for beach parties and great times with friends and family. Limbo dancing can also be easily replicated with equipment found in a home or school.

Turn on some upbeat music (*Beach Boys* if you have any) use a hockey stick or a broomstick and follow the rules provided below. Children will be looking at how everyday items can be used in different ways, getting active, and having fun!

1. A pole is held parallel to the ground by two people.

2. The students form a line and, in turn, they make their best effort to pass under the bar.

3. After everyone in the line has had their turn, the bar is lowered an inch or two and the students make an attempt at passing under the lowered bar again.

4. When passing under the bar, the students must bend backwards, no part of their bodies may touch the bar and the only part of their body that may touch the ground are their feet. Students are eliminated if they fall over, touch the bar or touch the ground.

5. As contestants are eliminated, the length between contestants' turns decreases and the level of their flexibility is progressively more challenged.

6. The winner is essentially the last person standing.

8) There's Something Fishy About this Activity

The underwater world has its own complex and wondrous environment. Fish inhabit both salt water and freshwater bodies of water.

Saltwater fish live in oceans and seas with salt water. Freshwater fish live in lakes, rivers, streams and rivers with fresh water.

Tropical fish can be found in fresh water and salt water. They include many wonderful colours and patterns.

Let young learners explore the underwater world in their imaginations by designing what 'they would consider' a beautiful tropical fish from their imagination.

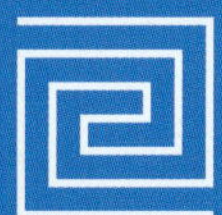

If you have a body of water near where you live, research with your child or class what kinds of fish live in it.

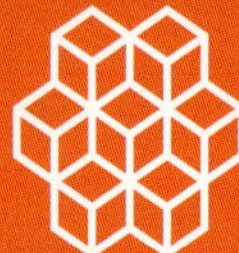

- Research Skills
- Artistic Skills

9) Dive into Cooking

The next three recipes are inspired by the beach and are easy to make together with your class or child.

Humming a Beach Tune-a

Tuna melts are a quick and delicious way for families to enjoy fish... the cheese is often an incentive to try something new.

Tuna Melt

You will need:

2 English muffins (4 halves)

1 can flaked tuna, drained

1-2 Tbsp light mayonnaise

salt and pepper to taste

1 cup shredded cheese

1. Preheat broiler in oven and spray a baking sheet with non-stick spray.

2. In a small bowl, combine tuna, mayonnaise, salt and pepper and mix well.

3. Spread tuna mixture on the English muffin halves and top with shredded cheese.

4. Place under the broiler for 3-5 minutes.

Note Minced onion is a great addition to the tuna spread, and sliced tomatoes between the tuna and the cheese is always delicious!

Ice Cream, Really Scream for the Beach

Ice cream is a favourite beach treat. The cupcake ice cream recipe included below provides the opportunity to replicate this delicious treat in a way that can be appreciated regardless of the weather.

Note In a classroom setting, you may wish to prepare the ice cream cupcakes in advance and have your students complete the decorating.

Ice Cream Cupcakes

You will need:

1 box cake mix (approx.18 ounce) plus additional ingredients listed on the box

24 flat-bottomed ice cream cones

2 tubs store bought icing or 2-3 cups homemade.

decorations (sprinkles, confetti and coloured chocolate buttons)

Steps:

1. Preheat oven to 350°F. Spray 2 muffin pans with non-stick spray.

2. Prepare cake batter as per the instructions on the box.

3. Stand ice cream cones in muffin cups and fill $2/3$ way with batter.

4. Bake for 15-20 minutes until a toothpick comes out clean.

5. Allow the cones to cool and then ice and decorate.

Makes 24 ice cream cupcakes

I Flip Flop for Fruit Punch

Here is a recipe for punch that will turn your meal into a real beach party!

Fruit Punch

You will need:

4 medium bananas

2 cups cold unsweetened pineapple juice

½ cup tropical punch-flavoured drink mix powder

2 cups cold orange juice

2 cups water

4 cups ice

Steps:

1. Place bananas and pineapple juice in blender container and cover.
2. Blend on high speed until well blended.
3. Measure drink mix into punch bowl or large pitcher.
4. Add orange juice and stir until drink mix is completely dissolved.
5. Add cold water and ice and stir.
6. Add banana mixture and stir until well blended.

Makes 8 servings, 1 cup each

Challenge There are a number of vegetables that grow in the sea, including Nori, Dulse, Arame, Sea Lettuce and Wakame. Take a field trip to the grocery store with your child or class and ask the green grocer what varieties are available. See how many you can find and examine. Find out which countries they come from.

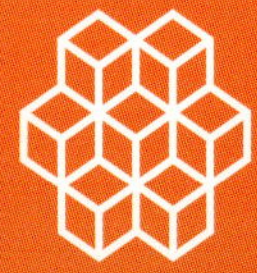

Building Blocks for Creativity

- Kitchen Skills
- Investigative Skills

10) **Boogie Without The** Bored

Encourage your class or child to throw their own beach party for their friends, family or another class! Have young learners make their own 'things to do list' from the activities below, and use it to create an actual party.

Activities to Consider

1. Decide who will be invited to the beach party and let them know about it.

2. Welcome each person with a Lei.

3. Serve beach party food.

4. Offer science and recreational activities.

5 Let guests re-build your sandcastle puzzle.

6. Boogie to beach music.

Building Blocks for Creativity

- Planning Skills
- Implementation Skills

It's So Easy
Being Green

We live in a time when reducing, reusing and recycling will hopefully become second nature to our children. If we can teach them to respect and take responsibility for the environment, we are truly helping to give them the world.

We did not inherit the earth from our parents, we are borrowing it from our children.
Native American Proverb

Creative IQ Goal

The activities below are meant to teach children how easy it is to make green living a part of their daily life. In addition, they develop children's ability to make positive choices in their life.

1) Re**Search**

Recycling is important if we want to reduce the amount of garbage in our world. This exercise involves teaching children how to identify recyclable items in their home or classroom, so that they can take part in putting them aside to be sent to the recycling depot.

Together with your children or students, sit down at your computer, visit your local school library or examine material supplied by your municipality, to determine together what kinds of materials are recyclable.

Have each child make a list of items commonly used in your home or classroom that can be recycled.

2) Re**Cook**

Parents can show children the importance of not wasting resources, including food, by using the same vegetables in different recipes. Children can help make each meal and see how prepared food can be used again in new and interesting ways. In a classroom, you may wish to make several meals over the course of one day.

A recipe has been included for roast vegetables, which can then be added to a pizza, pasta entree, rice or salad, or pureed into a soup.

Roasted Vegetables

This dish is easy to make and the ingredients are versatile.

It goes really well with roasted fish, chicken, steak and hamburgers, or on top of rice or pasta.

You will need:

8-12 cups in total of any of the following vegetables: baby carrots, cauliflower florets, sliced green or red peppers, halved mushrooms, sliced onions, sliced zucchini, sliced Chinese eggplant and brussel sprouts

2-4 Tbsp olive oil

salt and pepper to taste

Note For a little more flavour, feel free to add a sprinkle of any of these seasonings: basil, curry powder, garlic powder, rosemary or paprika.

Steps:

1. Preheat oven to 375°F; line a baking sheet with foil that has been sprayed with non-stick spray (depending on the quantity of vegetables you are using, you may require 3 baking sheets).

2. Wash, dry and cut up the vegetables.

3. Place the vegetables in a large bowl and sprinkle with olive oil, salt, pepper and any additional seasonings. Toss or stir so that they are well coated.

4. Spread the vegetables in a single layer on the prepared baking sheet (or sheets) and roast uncovered for 35-40 minutes.

5. When the vegetables are roasted, some may be slightly blackened around the edges.

6. Remove from the oven; place on a platter and serve.

Challenge Ask your child or class to brainstorm a list of foods that can be used in different meals: e.g., salmon → grilled entrée → sandwich filling → on top of a salad → tossed with pasta.

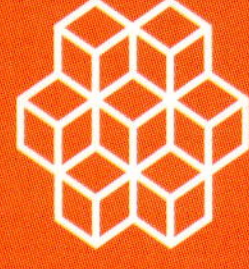

Building Blocks for Creativity
- Kitchen Skills
- Planning Skills

3) Re**Design**

Design a playhouse with your child or students out of an empty appliance box. Cut, draw, paint and make an *'original home or school-made'* toy together.

Challenge Let young learners create additional 'home or school-made' toys or sculptures from things in their recycling box.

Encourage children to choose items over a period of weeks, things that will let them develop their own make-believe grocery store or city. In a classroom setting, ask each child to bring in supplies from home to complete their project.

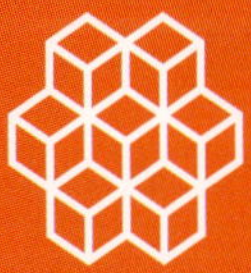

Building Blocks for Creativity
- Design Skills
- Innovative Thinking Skills

4) Re**Organize**

The word 'collage' means 'to glue.' A collage is made by gluing a variety of items to a base in order to create a new art form. These items can include paper, fabric, photographs, glass, foam or felt.

Through this next collage art project, children will find another great use for previously used magazines, newspapers and other materials.

Encourage children to go through old magazines and newspapers, collect scraps of material and some old family photos, flyers, and make a collage of things that best reflect who they are. In a classroom, you may ask children to bring in pictures and other materials in advance from home for the project.

You will need:

a piece of cardboard

pictures, paper and material scraps

scissors

paint brush (to apply the glue)

school glue

Steps:

1. Choose a piece of cardboard, which is suitable in both size and weight, to be the backing for your collage. Heavier material is better.

2. Collect the items you wish to include in your collage. Items like pictures from magazines or newspapers, photographs, or fancy paper work well.

3. Using a pair of scissors, cut out the items you plan to use and try arranging them on the cardboard backing. Sometimes tearing the paper produces an interesting jagged appearance. It is always better to plan before gluing.

4. Apply the glue to the back of the items and stick them onto the base. Let the glue dry.

Fun activity extension: Work with each child to turn their collage into a place mat. Cut clear/transparent paper just bigger than the collage, use white school glue on both sheets and "sandwich" the collage in between. Easy to clean!

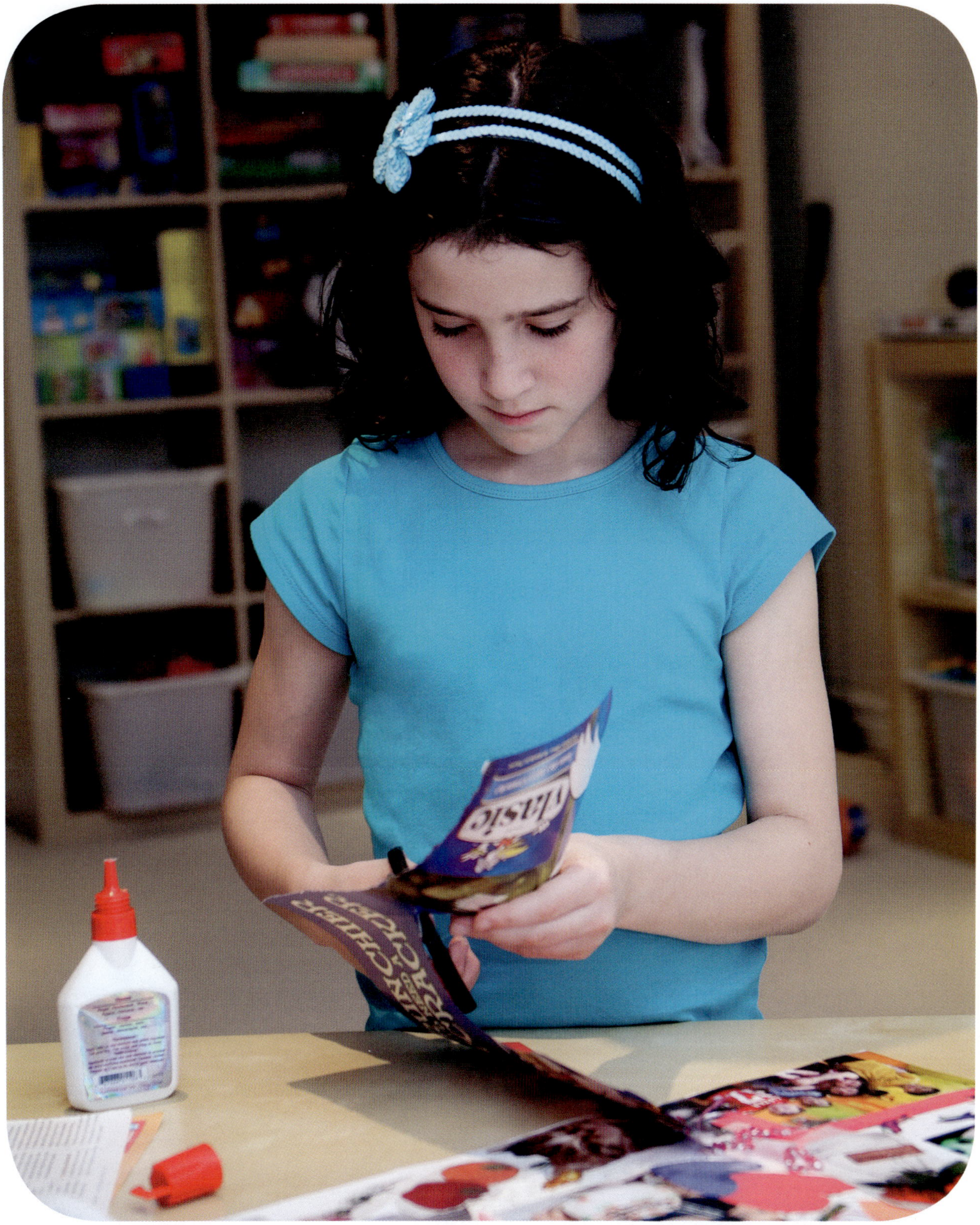

Ask children to describe why they used each picture or piece of material in their collage—giving them an opportunity to develop their verbal skills.

Questions for discussion may include:

a) What made each picture or material special to you?

b) How do you feel when you look at your completed collage?

c) What materials or pictures would you have added to your collage if you could find them?

d) What important characteristics or hobbies, which reflect you and your interests, are missing from your collage?

e) If you could re-make your collage, would you have chosen the same pictures and materials?

Building Blocks for Creativity

• Innovative Thinking Skills
• Verbal Skills

5) ReInvent

For parents and educators, part of living a greener life is teaching children to examine how things can be used (or re-used) in different ways. The following exercise is fun and effective in developing a child's ability to examine items with an open mind.

In the case of one child, present a variety of items and ask him or her to use each object in a different way than its intended purpose: e.g., a jar can be used as a drum, a pencil as a flute or a pot as a seat.

In a classroom setting, ask the children to sit in a circle and pass each item around, giving learners the chance to present a creative way to use the object in their own space (see examples above). You may choose to have the child explain what he or she is doing, or have the other children guess.

Building Blocks for Creativity

• Improvisation Skills
• Innovative Thinking Skills

6) Re**Create**

Let your students or children use old broken crayons to create colourful *Crayon Artwork*. This art project is a great way to get rid of the many little crayon pieces that you have lying around.

Have young learners read the instructions below that will help guide them in the activity.

Melted Crayon Art

You will need:

crayons

coloured pencils

blunt-tip scissors

recycled newspaper

iron (for adult use only!)

wax paper

pencil sharpener/ or cheese grater

Steps:

1. Draw various shapes or a picture on paper with coloured pencils.

2. Cover a flat work area that is safe for ironing with several layers of recycled newspaper. Place the sheet of paper with your picture on it and top it with a piece of wax paper (so your picture is visible from below).

3. With adult supervision, scrape crayons into small pieces using a pencil sharpener or place them in a resealable bag and crush them with a rolling pin.

4. Scatter the crayon colors around the wax paper. Place another sheet of wax paper on top.

5. Ask an adult to iron the two pieces together, melting the crayons. Cool.

Note Ironing should only be done on a low heat by an adult.

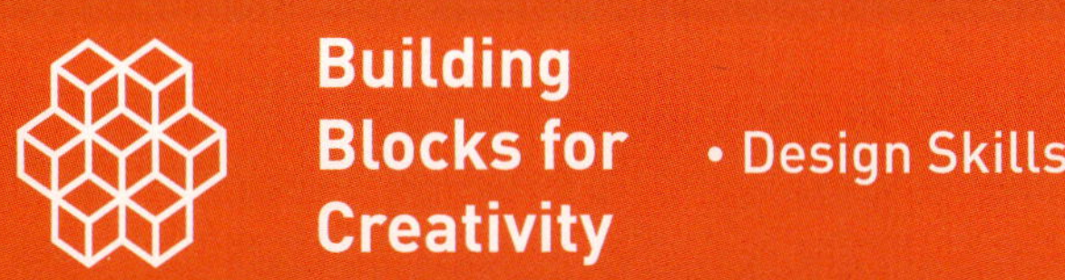

7) Re**Harmonize**

Have your child create one or more new musical instrument using items from your kitchen cupboards, recycling box, or classroom supplies cupboard, rather than resorting to a manufacturing process; e.g., drums from pots or sand pails, shakers from bottles filled with pasta, blowing across bottles with different levels of water.

Challenge

Let children create a band using their instrument(s) with you or in classroom groups. Have them choose a name for the band. Record the music on audio or video camera, and invite others to come and listen to their *concert*.

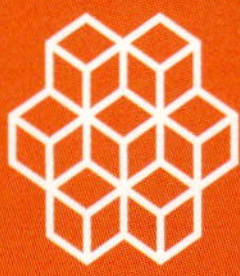

Building Blocks for Creativity

• Brainstorming Skills
• Musical Appreciation Skills

8) Re**Gift**

Brainstorm with children about how they can recycle in new ways in your home: e.g., give away or donate old clothes, books and toys.

Challenge Organize a book or toy exchange together with young learners, an activity they can enjoy with their friends or other students at school.

Have children consider with you the 'to do list' below in preparation for the event.

To Do List for Book or Toy Exchange

a) Choose a date, time and place for the exchange. Ensure that the room or facility is available.

b) Decide who will be invited to the exchange and how they will be informed: i.e., by e-mail or posters.

c) Plan how, when, and where the items for the exchange will be brought by participants in order to make it easier to organize.

d) Figure out the number of people required to co-ordinate the exchange, how it will take place and in what way the instructions will be given to the children or students.

e) Make a list of what needs to happen on the day of the exchange from set-up to clean-up.

f) Assign roles in advance to ensure that all steps happen smoothly.

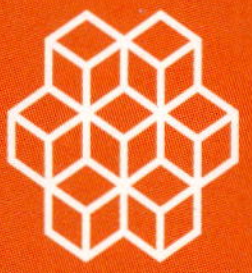

Building Blocks for Creativity

• Brainstorming Skills
• Planning Skills

9) Re**Write**

Have young learners create an *environmental e-newspaper* that can be scanned or typed into the computer, to share with family, friends and/or other students via e-mail. Include research, artwork and experiences from the activities in this chapter.

In a classroom setting, you may wish to divide the students into groups to create material for the newspaper

Note This newspaper could be the first edition of a monthly e-newspaper to share green initiatives with friends or others in the school.

Challenge Visit a local recycling depot with your child or class, and have them interview an employee for one of the *e-newspaper* articles, with questions prepared in advance and on-the-spot.

Interview questions may include:

a) What does recycling mean to you?

b) What are the benefits of recycling?

c) Which materials are recyclable?

d) Where are recyclable materials collected?

e) How and where are recyclable materials sorted?

f) What steps in the recycling process take place at this recycling plant?

g) What government requirements must your plant meet for recycling?

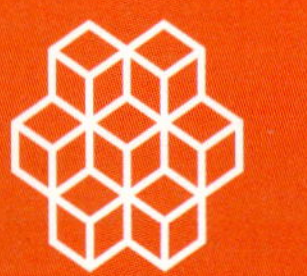

Building Blocks for Creativity

• Creative Writing Skills
• Interviewing Skills

10) ReDiscover

Play a hide-and-seek game with children to help them learn to find metal recyclables.

In this activity, you will be hiding a variety of small metal objects in sand or rice, e.g., a paper clip or nickel, and letting children use a magnet to try and find the items.

You will need:

a reusable plastic container

sand or rice

some small metal items (to include: nickels, paper clips, dimes, bottle tops)

a magnet

Steps:

1. Fill the container (half full) with the sand or rice.

2. Hide the metal items.

3. Let children find the metal items using the magnet.

Building Blocks for Creativity

• Investigative Skills

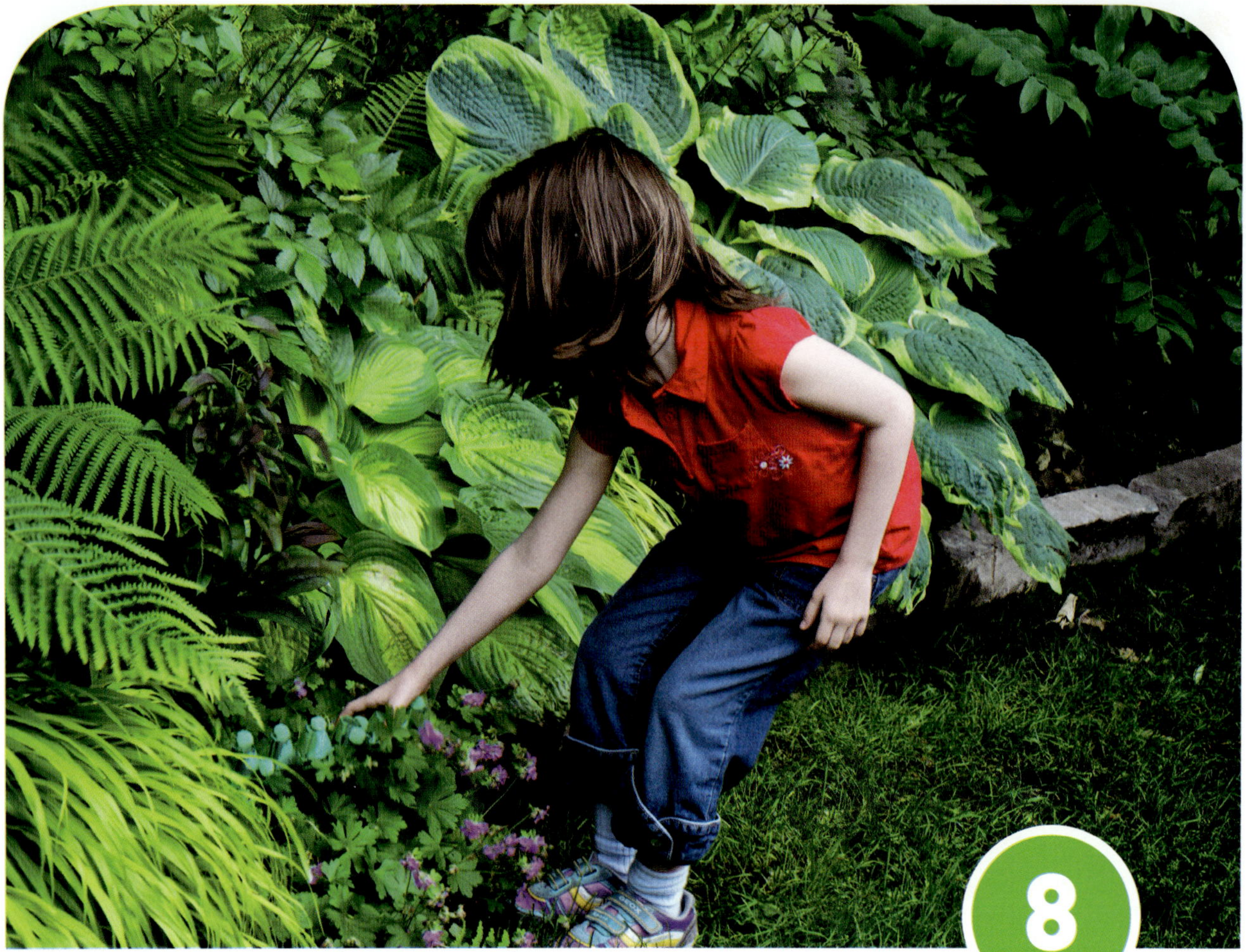

8

Say KNOW to

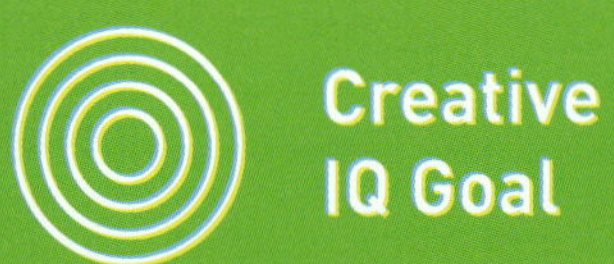

Insects and Bugs

Children are either fascinated or terrified by insects and bugs, much like their parents. This chapter takes a closer look at creepy crawlies and attempts to help the children overcome any present fears through education and experience.

Creative IQ Goal

By learning about insects and bugs, young learners can gain a better appreciation for nature and life, and lessen their fear of the unknown.

1) Who Really Bugs Me?

We tend to classify more creepy crawlies as insects than actually fall within the designation.

Discuss the key factors that identify insects with your child or class:

a)   one pair of antennae or feelers

b)   three pairs of legs

c)   three body parts (head, thorax and abdomen)

d)   an exoskeleton (its skeleton is on the outside), and

e)   there are also two pairs of wings, if any.

Then examine the diagrams below with the young learners and ask them to decide which of the pictured critters are insects, asking them to discuss how they reached their answers.

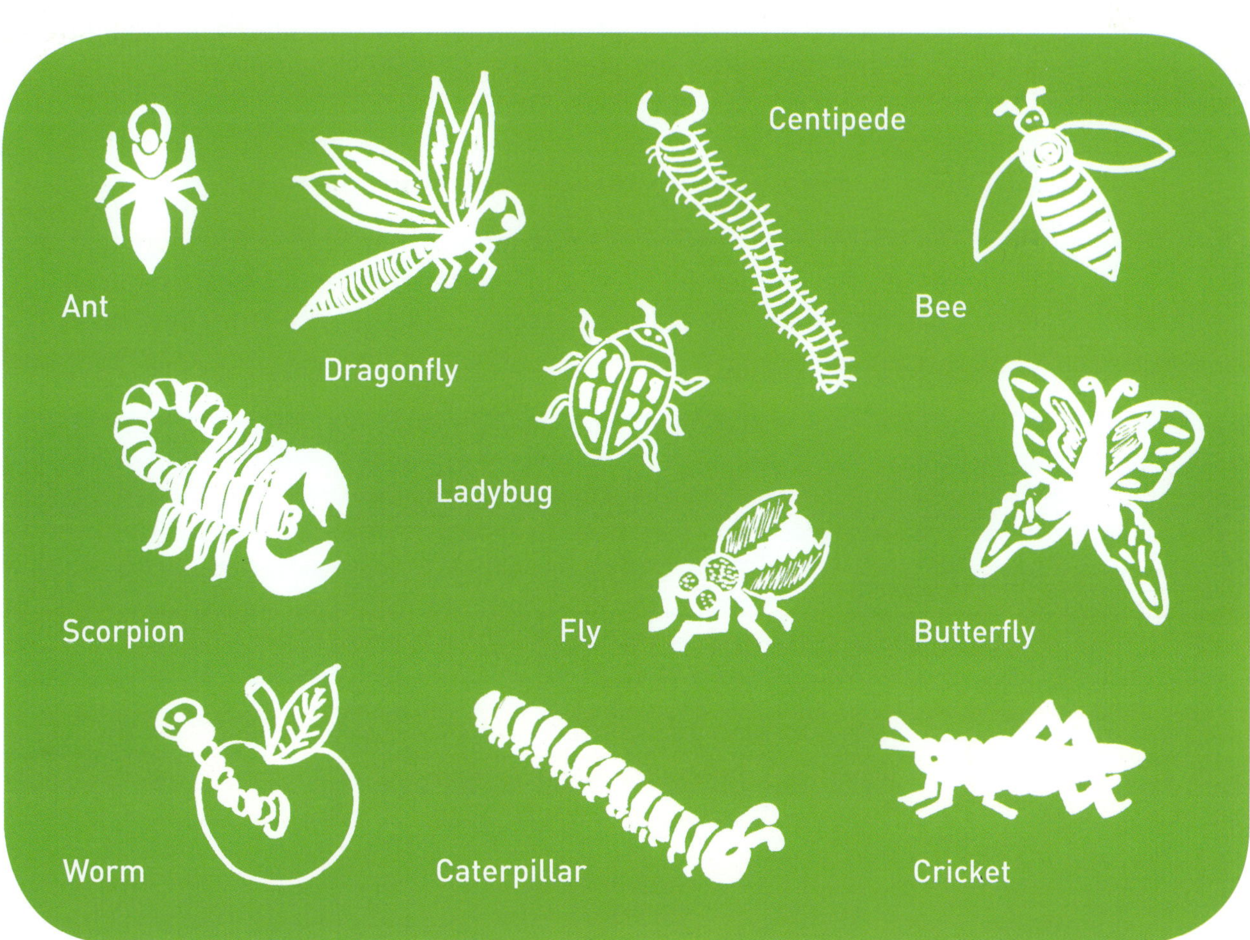

The following critters pictured above are insects: caterpillar, ant, dragonfly, bee, ladybug, butterfly, fly, cricket.

2) The Very Hungry Me

The Very Hungry Caterpillar by Eric Carle is a wonderful easy-to-read board book that teaches children about numbers, days of the week, and the process of changing from a caterpillar to a butterfly. Young children love poking their fingers through the holes in the board book, where the 'caterpillar has taken bites' out of food.

Obtain a copy of *The Very Hungry Caterpillar* to read as part of this next exercise. The activity involves gathering the food referenced in the book as eaten by the caterpillar, for your class or child to sample.

Become a lean, green, eating machine

Read *The Very Hungry Caterpillar* together and then enjoy a fun taste test of the foods you have collected, as young learners pretend they are caterpillars. It can be a great role playing exercise, and a chance to try new foods.

Challenge Ask each child to describe their favourite foods, and then list and draw pictures of them as though their choices were used as a page in *The Very Hungry Caterpillar* book. The exercise allows young learners to become a storyteller as well.

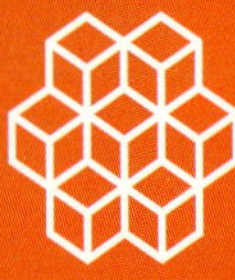

3) Super Insect Power: Camouflage

Camouflage allows insects to become virtually invisible as they blend into their environment. It is an excellent way to hide from their predators and enemies.

Let your child or class create their own insect that can camouflage itself inside your home, classroom, garden or nearby park, using art supplies or recycled materials. The insect models should include the defining components already discussed in the first activity.

Instructions for Creating a Camouflaged Insect

You will need:

egg cartons

paper towel rolls

pipe cleaners

tissue and construction paper

paint, in assorted camouflage colours

school glue

a pair of scissors

Steps:

1. Show the children examples and pictures of insect camouflage.

2. Allow each child to use the art supplies to create their very own insects.

3. Have the children take their insects outside and camouflage or hide them in their environment.

4. See if you can find the camouflaged insects.

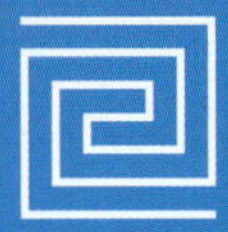

Challenge Have children research online those insects that camouflage or blend into their environment.

Questions for research or discussion may include:

a) Find examples of insects that use camouflage.

a) How does an insect camouflage itself?

b) Discuss the benefits of an insect being able to camouflage itself.

c) What effect do seasonal changes have on camouflage?

d) What is mimicry? How does it differ from camouflage?

Building Blocks for Creativity
• Puzzle Solving Skills
• Reading Skills

4) In Sections of the Park I go

Your child or class can have the chance to get close and personal with insects in their own community. Go on an insect search and try to find and observe as many different kinds as possible.

Challenge

Bring a notebook and crayons along, and ask each child to draw pictures of the insects he or she sees. When you return have the children try to identify the particular insects seen, using books or canvassing the Internet.

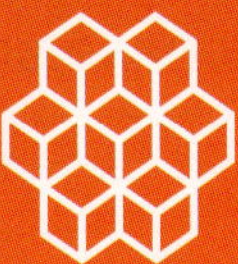

Building Blocks for Creativity

- Comparison Skills
- Observation Skills

5) Butterflies and Spiders for Picky Eaters

Below are recipes for butterfly cupcakes and spider cookies, which should appeal to picky and non-picky eaters. Have a '*snail*' of a time making them together or bring them into your classroom for snack time.

Butterfly Cupcakes

You will need:

1 package cake mix, plus the ingredients to prepare the mix

1 container vanilla icing

blue and green food colouring

assorted candies for decorating

coloured sugar

red liquorice strings, cut into 4-inch pieces

1. Preheat oven to 350°F. Lightly spray 2 standard size muffin pans with non-stick spray.

2. Prepare cake mix according to the directions on the package. Spoon batter in the prepared muffin cups, filling all 24 cups.

3. Bake the "cupcakes" for 20-22 minutes. Remove cupcakes from the muffin pan and allow to cool completely on a wire rack.

4. Divide the icing equally between 2 bowls. Add a few drops of each of the food colouring to each bowl, a drop at a time, until you reach the desired shade. Stir the icing well.

5. Cut the top off the cupcake, and cut the cupcake top in half. Place the cupcake halves together with the cut sides facing out, to resemble butterfly wings. Ice with the desired colours.

6. Decorate with assorted candies and coloured sugar.

7. Trim each piece of liquorice string to form the butterfly's antennae and place in the centre of each cupcake.

Makes 24 cupcakes

Spider cookies

Per spider you will need:

2 oatmeal or chocolate chip cookies

1 Tbsp of vanilla icing

red shoestring licorice

2 chocolate candy-coated buttons

Steps:

1. Spread icing on the flat sides of both cookies.

2. Break red licorice laces into 4 long pieces or 8 short pieces.

3. Place the licorice "legs" across one of the cookies so they stick out to look like legs.

4. Place the other cookie on top.

5. Spread icing over the top cookie and top it with two chocolate buttons, to look like eyes.

Makes 1 very sweet but scary spider

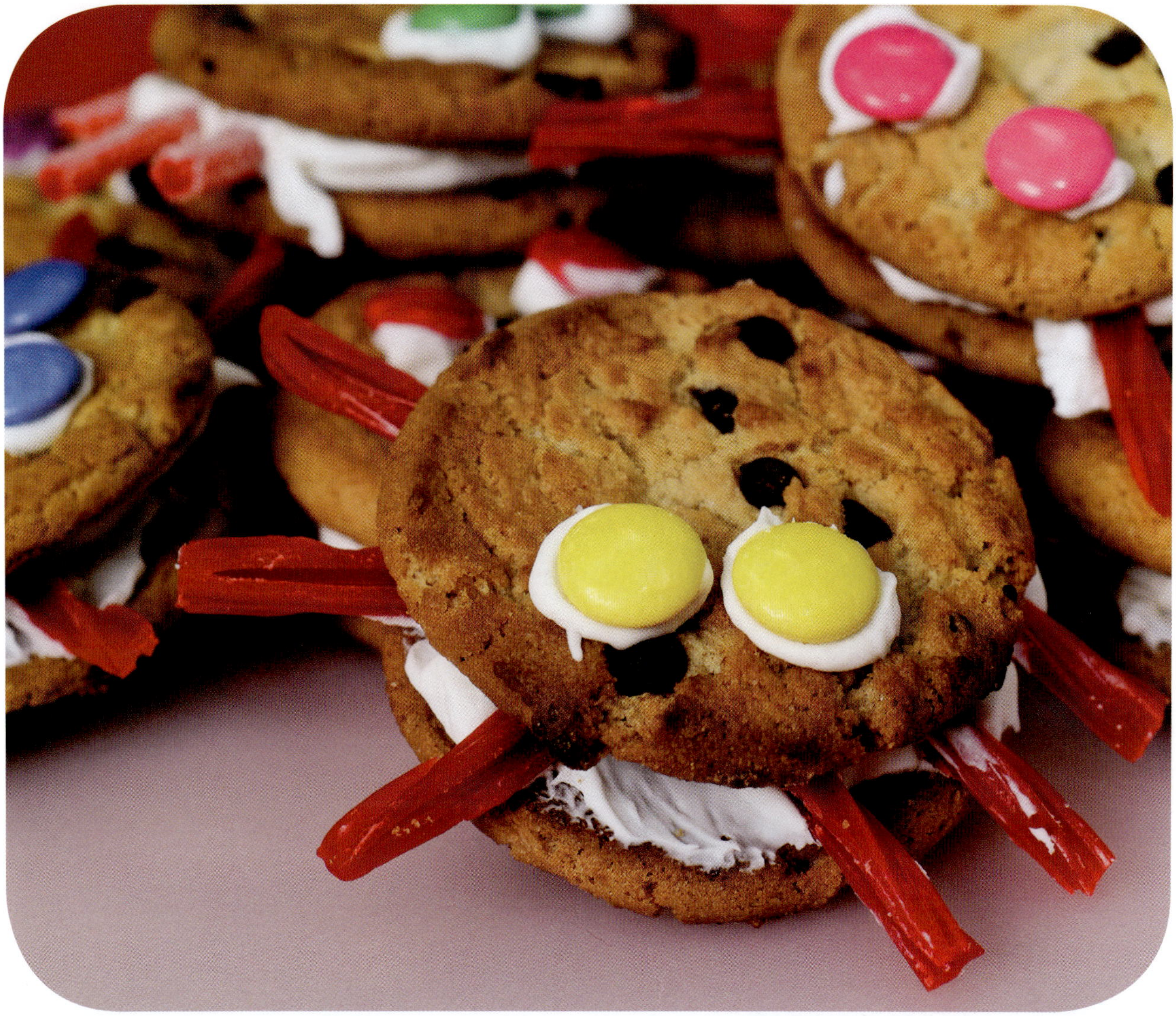

Do some research with your child or students about bugs that are safely eaten around the world. Then give them the option to create a menu for a restaurant serving bugs in their food.

- Kitchen Skills
- Innovative Thinking Skills

6) Let's Get Buggy

You can easily create a game for your child or class to play, one that lets them practice everything they have learned about insects, while still having fun.

Put together thirty pictures of different insects drawn or printed from the Internet.

The game will be played by pairs of players as follows:

1. Each player takes fifteen cards without looking at them.

2. Player One will hold up a picture above their head without looking at it and Player Two will describe the insect without saying what it is.

3. Player One has to guess the insect on their own card.

4. Then Player Two will hold up a picture in the same way and let player One describe it.

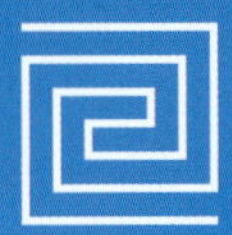

Challenge Your child or students can now make their own 'Insect Memory Game' to play with their friends.

1. Present each child with ten or more paper squares, cut exactly the same size.

2. Have each child draw pairs of insects.

3. The game is played by mixing up the pieces of paper, and placing them facing down on the floor. The first player turns over two squares. If she finds a match, she gets another turn. If there is no match, the other player gets a turn.

4. The person who discovers the most matches wins.

Building Blocks for Creativity
- Verbal Skills
- Memory Skills

7) Fly Me Away

This activity gives your students or child the opportunity to consider what it would feel like to be a fly.

Ask each child to consider the following scenario:

You are a fly! Your best friend, another fly, just got caught in a spider's web.

a) Then ask young learners to write a story about how she would save her friend.

b) Have each child draw one or more pictures to illustrate their story.

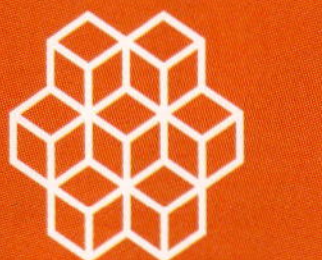

Building Blocks for Creativity
- Creative Writing Skills
- Artistic Skills

8) Fly Me to Your Paints

Butterfly wings are symmetrical, or identical to each other in shape and colour.

Your child or students will have the chance to create their own mirror image wings, using paint and butterfly paper cut-outs.

Instructions for Creating a Symmetrical Butterfly

You will need:

a sheet of cardboard, Bristol board or construction paper

pencil

a pair of scissors

a variety of paint colours

paintbrushes

1. Fold a piece of cardboard in half vertically, and using the fold as the middle of the butterfly, draw the outline of half of a butterfly and one wing on the cardboard sheet with a pencil.

2. Cut out the butterfly shape and open up the cardboard to reveal a symmetrical butterly.

3. Paint one side or one wing with a generous amount of paint.

4. Fold the one wing over the other and press down hard.

5. Note how the pattern that appears on both sides is exactly the same.

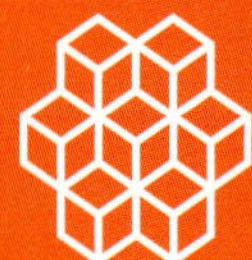

Building Blocks for Creativity • Artistic Skills

9) Bee a Spider Designer

Spiders have eight legs. Imagine if they had to shop for clothes! Just for fun, ask each child to design eight spider shoes.

Challenge

The Itsy-Bitsy Spider is a famous nursery rhyme. Ask each child to create a new nursery rhyme about their spider in his or her new shoes; young learners can either change some of the words in the famous version or create an original rhyme.

Below is an example of a rhyme created by changing the words of the famous version:

The spider in his sneakers climbed up the water spout,

Down came the rain, and he quickly ran right out,

Out came the sun, so he could run again,

And the itsy-bitsy spider raced up the spout again.

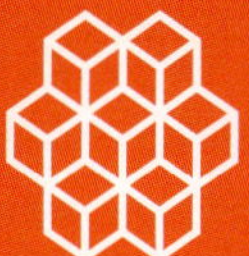

Building Blocks for Creativity

- Design Skills
- Creative Writing Skills

10) **Flight of Your** Bumblebee

Flight of the Bumblebee, an orchestral interlude written by Nikolai Rimsky-Korsakov, easily inspires images of busy bumblebees flying, gathering nectar or pollen from flowering plants, and socializing with other bees.

Find a recording of *Flight of the Bumblebee* to share with your child or class.

Then ask the young learners to close their eyes and listen to the song, imagining bumblebees in their mind. After the piece is done, have the children move as if they were bumblebees as you play *Flight of the Bumblebee* for them again.

Note *Flight of the Bumblebee* is available at www.YouTube.com, played on a variety of instruments.

Building Blocks for Creativity

- Musical Appreciation Skills
- Improvisation Skills

Fruit**astic Fun**

An understanding of nutrition can help children appreciate the benefits of healthy eating habits. We have developed fruit-astic fun to give meaning to the expression 'you are what you eat.'

Creative IQ Goal

The activities in this chapter are designed to help your child or students understand the importance of analyzing the benefits of a product, project or goal. In this case attention is centered on the various kinds of fruit.

1) Do you Feel Fruity?

What makes a fruit a *fruit*?

A fruit is the ripe, edible and fleshy part that covers the seed of a plant.

The most well-known debate over fruit asks whether a tomato is a fruit or a vegetable. If one were to look at the definition of a fruit, it would say that if it has seeds it is a fruit. Tomatoes, although technically a fruit, are considered by most to be a vegetable. They are used in cookery as a vegetable.

Now ask children to go through the list of items provided below, and circle the food items that are fruit.

Food Items:

artichoke	eggplant	raisins
avocado	garlic	rhubarb
beets	guavas	romaine lettuce
broccoli	lemons	rutabaga
carrots	parsnips	tomatoes
cherries	pears	water chestnuts
cherry tomatoes	peppers	watermelon
corn	plums	cucumber
cranberries	prunes	zucchini

Answers:

Fruits

avocado	guavas	raisins
cherries	lemons	tomatoes
cherry tomatoes	pears	watermelon
cranberries	peppers	zucchini
cucumber	plums	
eggplant	prunes	

Vegetables

artichokes	corn	romaine lettuce
beets	garlic	rutabaga
broccoli	parsnips	water chestnuts
carrots	rhubarb	

Building Blocks for Creativity • Critical Thinking Skills

2) Olive **to Play Guessing Games**

Children can test their knowledge of fruit, as well as develop their comprehension skills, by reading the short descriptions of a fruit, and then choosing the fruit from four options (a, b, c or d) that best matches the description.

What am I?

Below are a series of descriptions for you to read and identify together with young learners.

1. I am a round tree fruit which has crisp white flesh, There are more than 100 varieties of me in North America. I can vary in colour from yellow to green to red. I have seeds at my centre which is protected by my core.

    What am I?

    a) pear   b) apple   c) peach

2. I am small, tart and sweet. You can find me growing in places like forests or fields. I grow in the late summer and early autumn, have a bright red colour and come in a pale yellow variety too.

    What am I?

    a) blueberry   b) gooseberry   c) raspberry

3. I have a smooth, creamy, greenish-yellow flesh with an unusually high amount of a healthy fat that is primarily monounsaturated. I have a pit in the middle and a skin that ranges form light to dark green depending on my variety.

    What am I?

    a) avocado   b) banana   c) cucumber

4. I am covered with a rough rind on the outside and have a delicious, sweet orange flesh on the inside. I am very nutritious and round like a ball in shape.

    What am I?

    a) watermelon   b) cantaloupe   c) honeydew

5. I am sweet and people drink me all the time to quench their thirst. I have a very high concentration of vitamins and minerals that our bodies need for good health. Even my peel is used in cooking.

What am I?

a) strawberry   b) orange   c) lime

6. I originate from China, the Philippines and India. I am a delectable fruit which is eaten fresh, canned or dried. My white fleshy tissue, once peeled from its hard, brown spiky shell, is sweet, fragrant and delicious.

What am I?

a) lychee   b) kumquat   c) dragon fruit

Answers

1. b   2. c   3. a   4. b   5. b   6. a

Challenge Have each child find fruit facts online, and make up their own question and answer guessing game for you.

Instructions for constructing a question:

a) Find fruit facts for fruit that will be the accurate answer to their question.

b) Choose two other fruits which share one, but not all of the characteristics or facts with the correct answer, to confuse the guesser.

c) Write out the question, and include the correct answer, and the two similar fruits as a, b and c.

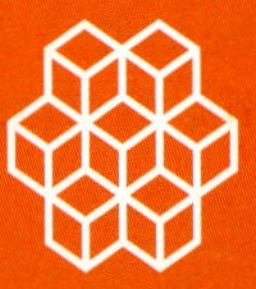

Building Blocks for Creativity • Analytical Skills

3) Dragon Fruit
Super Heroes (and More) ...

Children will enjoy an opportunity to learn more about the nutritional value of fruit, and their quasi 'super hero' qualities in this next activity. They will then communicate what they have learned in one or more creative ways.

Have children work individually or in groups to research the "super powers" of one of the fruit characters listed below at the library or on the Internet, to create a superhero profile. Each child or group will then use the information found to create a poster featuring the fruit and its "super powers" to present to you or their classmates.

Superhero character examples to choose from (or let children create their own names): Arthur Apple, Bailey Banana, Barry Blueberry, Stanley Strawberry, Rufus Raspberry, Barney Blackberry, Danny Date, Carly Cantaloupe, Wendy Watermelon, Hannah Honeydew, Natasha Nectarine, Penelope Peach, Melissa Mango, Oscar Orange, or Parker Pineapple.

Super Power Research Questions to Consider

a) What vitamins does your fruit contain?

b) Is your fruit a good source of fibre?

c) Does eating the fruit lower the risk of any particular diseases?

d) Is your fruit particularly healthy for a certain organ(s) in the body?

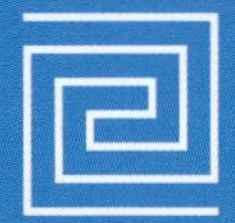

Challenge ONE

Have each child *design a Fruit Super Hero*, giving it a face, arms, legs, etc. The fruit figure could be performing an action as part of a picture, e.g., kicking a ball, playing the piano, skipping, singing and so forth. Have him or her colour the picture.

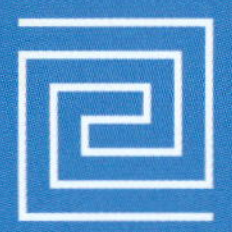

Challenge TWO

Ask each child to *create a comic strip* using their Fruit Super Hero.

Challenge THREE

Encourage each child to *create a short skit*, either alone or with other children, one of whom will be taking on the role of the Fruit Super Hero.

Building Blocks for Creativity

- Creative Writing Skills
- Improvisation Skills
- Artistic Skills

4) Be a Fruit Sleuth

The next activity encourages children to use their five senses to learn about new fruit, and to develop a better understanding of the grocery store and where fruit comes from.

Take young learners to the supermarket to see what unusual fruit they can "spy." Examine together where the fruits come from (by reading the signs or stickers), select a few of the fruits to buy, bring them home and taste them.

In a classroom setting, you may wish to modify the activity, by visiting an online grocery website together, such as www.grocerygateway.com, and creating a list of unusual fruit. Then ask the parents/children to sign up to bring in the different fruits for an 'in class' taste test.

Challenge

Ask children to use their senses to *describe* each fruit. You can explain that their *describing words* are also known as *adjectives*.

Questions to Create Sensory Fruit Descriptions:

a) What does each fruit smell like?

b) What does each fruit taste like?

c) How does each fruit feel in your hands or mouth or what is its texture?

d) Look at the fruit, and describe its shape and colour.

Building Blocks for Creativity

- Investigative Skills
- Sensory Skills
- Observation Skills

5) Can You Run Berry Fast?

In order to build a positive association with fruit, have young learners create their own Olympic games using fruit, something intended to amuse and enlighten their friends or family. As always, it starts with a 'to do' list.

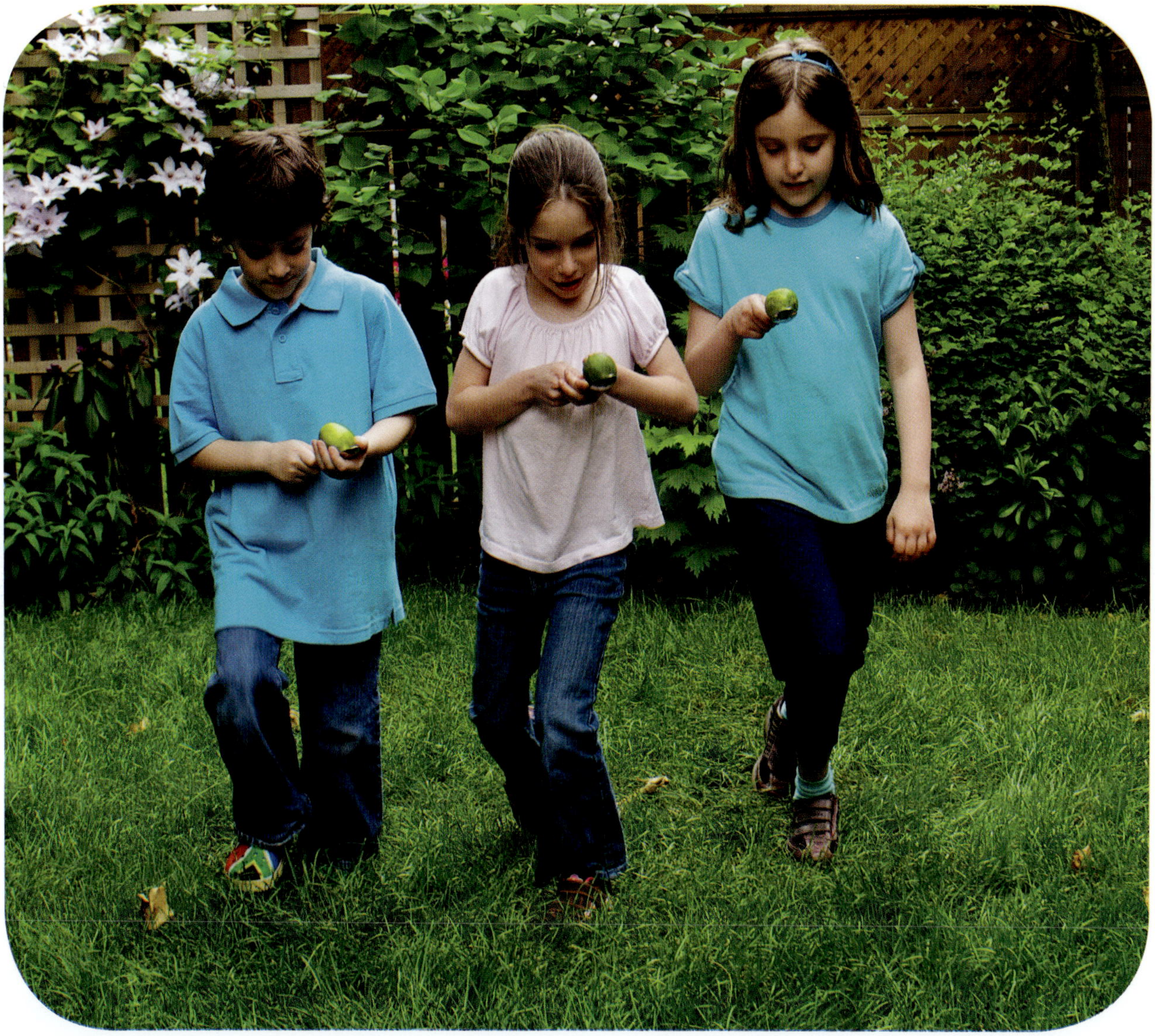

Sample 'To do' list for children:

a) Use your imagination to make up Olympic fruit activities. Events could include a Banana Relay, Strawberry on a Spoon Race, Plum Juggling or Apple Dunking.

b) Make up a grocery list for the games.

c) Create and send invitations to Olympic Fruit Athletes, including any relevant preparatory or game-day instructions. Note: In a classroom, the students may choose to be the Olympic Fruit Athletes.

d) Assign roles for Olympic preparations and the Olympic Day.

e) Make signs for different events.

f) Create advertisements or e-mail invitations (try www.evite.com) to attract guests to the Olympics.

Then have the children carry out their 'to do' list to create an actual Fruit Olympics.

Challenge   Ask children to write up one or more newspaper articles to describe their Fruit Olympics-related stories.

Remind young learners to include the 5 W's and 1 H of journalism when writing their article:

a) What happened?

b) Where did it happen?

c) When did it happen?

d) Why did it happen?

e) Who was involved?

f) How did it happen?

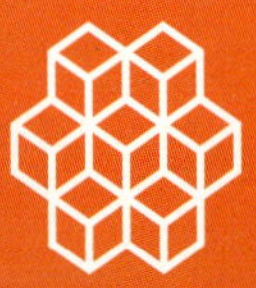

Building Blocks for Creativity
- Interpersonal Skills
- Phyical Fitness Skills
- Creative Writing Skills

6) I Con**seed** it! Cooking with Fruit is Fun

Below are recipes for Fruit Kebabs and Fruit Smoothies, which use fruit as the main ingredient.

Fruit Kebabs

You will need:

a variety of fruit cut into bite sized pieces

wooden skewers

vanilla or flavoured yogurt

a variety of cereals or cookies

re-sealable bag

1. Cut a variety of fruit into cubes or bite-sized pieces and thread onto wooden skewers.
2. Pour yogurt into a rectangular dish.
3. Place a variety of cereal or cookies into a large re-sealable bag, press out as much air as possible, seal and crush with a rolling pin.
4. Pour crumbs into another rectangular dish.
5. Finally, roll the fruit kebob in the yogurt and then in the cereal.

Fruit Smoothies

You will need:

1/3 cup pineapple or orange juice

1 cup fresh fruit (pineapple, blueberries, strawberries, mango, raspberries)

1 ripe banana

1/3 cup yogurt (or for a thicker smoothie use frozen yogurt or ice cream)

1 Tbsp honey, optional

Steps:

1. Cut up all of the fruit into chunks.
2. Place all of the ingredients in the blender and put the lid on firmly.
3. Blend until the mixture is smooth.
4. Pour into a big glass and drink.

Banana Chocolate Smoothie (for the more picky eaters!)

You will need:

1/2 cup milk (skim, 1% or 2%)

1 banana

1/2 cup vanilla frozen yogurt or vanilla ice cream

1 Tbsp chocolate chips

Steps:

Follow instructions above.

7) Spicing Things Up
Apple Cinnamon Play Dough

Apple Cinnamon play dough will not only provide children with the chance to build and design, but create a scent that may encourage them to ask, 'please cut me up an apple.'

Below is a recipe for Apple Cinnamon Play Dough to make and enjoy together.

You will need:

1 re-sealable bag

1 cup of ground cinnamon

1 cup of apple sauce

Steps:

1. In a re-sealable bag, combine equal quantities of ground cinnamon and apple sauce.

2. Seal the bag and use your hands to move it around until it becomes the texture of play dough.

3. When the ingredients are completely combined, remove the dough from the bag and create something you can put on the windowsill in your kitchen or classroom that will leave the room smelling delicious!

8) Fruit Apeels in Many Ways

The next activity encourages children to brainstorm the different ways we can enjoy the same fruit.

Ask each child to pick a favourite fruit and to make a list of how many ways it can be cooked and eaten. For example, an apple can be dried, made into sauce, grated into muffins, pressed into juice, and chopped or tossed in a garden salad or fruit salad.

Questions to consider may include:

a) Does your fruit grow from a plant, tree or vine?

b) Describe how the fruit grows.

c) What kind of environment and weather conditions are required for its growth?

d) What time of year is it picked or harvested?

9) Figure out the Dried Fruit

Fruits look and taste different when they are dried.

Raisins, once grapes when ripe, provide a great visual example of how different fruits can look when they are dried.

Place a few grapes and raisins on a plate in front of young learners. Explain to the children that raisins are dried grapes. Then ask the children to describe the differences they observe between the grapes and raisins.

Fruit Drying Experiment

The experiment below will give children the opportunity to observe the gradual changes in the texture and size of the fruit during the drying process, and take note of the time required for it to be completed.

You will need:

either ½ cup grapes, 2-3 apricots or 1 apple

large brown paper bags

notebook for observations

pencil

Steps:

1) Cut open a brown paper bag so that it lays flat.

2) Spread the grapes out on the paper bag.

3) Place the bag in the sunlight where it will not be disturbed.

4) Using a pencil or marker, draw a line around the outline of each piece of fruit.

5) Take a notebook and write down the children's observations every 1-2 days for a two week period, recording the date with each entry. Observations should record the size, colour, shape and texture of the fruit.

Note Do not have children eat the dried fruit from the experiment.

Purchase and provide young tasters with samples of the fresh and dried version of each fruit on plates. Then have the children:

a) Guess the ripe fruit on the table from which each dried fruit came.

b) Taste the dry and ripe versions of each fruit and describe the differences in their taste.

Examples of dried fruits which may be used include: apples, cranberries, raisins, prunes, kiwi, pineapple, coconut, apricot, and mango.

10) Er (air), Why Does Fruit Brown?

Apples, bananas, pears and other produce turn brown when cut because the cutting or bruising damages the fruit cells, causing an enzyme in the fruit to react with oxygen and other chemicals in the air. The browning process can be slowed down in a number of ways, for example, by adding an acid such as lemon juice to the fruit.

An experiment has been provided below to examine how long it takes fruit to turn brown, with and without lemon on top.

Fruit Browning Experiment

You will need:

fruit that browns when cut, such as apples, apricots or peaches

freshly squeezed lemon juice

plates labelled one and two

notebook for observations

pencils

pencil crayons or crayons

Steps:

1) Cut fresh fruit into slices, and divide them equally between the two plates labelled one and two.

2) Sprinkle lemon juice on the fruit slices on plate number two.

3) Ask children to write down in words and/or to draw the amount of browning that has taken place on the fruit slices on each of plate #1 and plate #2, every ten minutes for one hour.

4) Have children compare the length of time it takes the fruit slices to brown with or without lemon juice, and describe their conclusions orally or in writing.

Challenge ONE

Have children repeat the experiment with other varieties of fruits, and compare differences in browning times between the fruits with and without lemon.

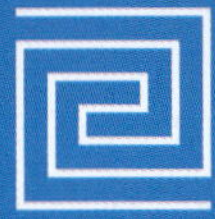

Challenge TWO

Ask children to research online other methods for slowing the browning process in cut produce and present their results, e.g., heating the cut fruit through cooking or submerging the cut fruit in water or vacuum-sealing the cut fruit. You may then ask children to test some of the other methods discovered in order to put their findings into action, with adequate adult supervision where required for safety.

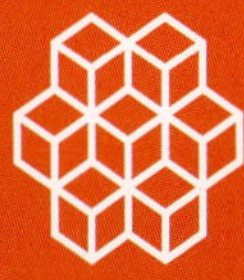

Building Blocks for Creativity

- Science Skills
- Comparison Skills

A Camping
We Will Go!

Camping-themed activities provide a fun way to expose children to the 'natural' world around them. It could also build excitement for a future family vacation in the great outdoors.

Creative IQ Goal

The primary focus of this chapter is to develop young learners' appreciation of nature and their awareness of the environment.

1) Canoe Guess the Food?

The special foods associated with outings or trips, such as baseball games (popcorn), carnivals (cotton candy) and the beach (ice cream) become part of the experience. In this activity, you will examine typical camping foods together with the children.

Blind fold each child (taking turns in a classroom setting) and have him or her try to guess what common camping foods they are trying. This exercise is not only fun, it also encourages kids to try new foods, and demonstrates how one sense is heightened (taste), when another sense is taken away (sight).

Some common camping foods include: baked beans, oatmeal, hotdogs, marshmallows, trail mix, macaroni, pancakes, chilli, S'mores, stews, soups, hamburgers and corn on the cob.

Building Blocks for Creativity

- Analytical Skills
- Sensory Skills

2) I'm Going on a Word Hunt

Many special camping experiences are not bought or held. In fact, they come alive through our appreciation of them; e.g., looking for interesting plants, our first canoe ride.

We have provided three camping and safety messages below for children to *search and find*.

How? Each letter of the alphabet is assigned a number. Children need to find the letter that corresponds to the number in order to uncover the hidden messages.

a - 1	g - 7	l - 12	q - 17	v - 22
b - 2	h - 8	m - 13	r - 18	w - 23
c - 3	i - 9	n - 14	s - 19	x - 24
d - 4	j - 10	o - 15	t - 20	y - 25
e - 5	k - 11	p - 16	u - 21	z - 26
f - 6				

1. __ __ __ __ __   __ __ __ __ __ __ __   __ __   __ __
   7 15 9 14 7   3 1 13 16 9 14 7   9 19   19 15

   __ __ __ __   __ __ __
   13 21 3 8   6 21 14

2. __ __   __ __ __   __ __ __   __ __ __ __ __ __   __ __ __
   23 5   3 1 14   19 9 20   1 18 15 21 14 4   20 8 5

   __ __ __ __ __ __ __   __ __ __   __ __ __ __   __ __ __ __ __
   3 1 13 16 6 9 18 5   1 14 4   19 9 14 7   19 15 14 7 19

3. __ __ __   __ __ __   __ __ __ __   __ __ __ __ __ __ __ __
   16 21 20   15 21 20   25 15 21 18   3 1 13 16 6 9 18 5

   __ __ __ __   __ __ __   __ __ __   __ __ __ __
   23 8 5 14   25 15 21   1 18 5   4 15 14 5

Answers

1. Going camping is so much fun
2. We can sit around the campfire and sing songs
3. Put out your campfire when you are done

Challenge

Children can make up their own hidden messages for their parents or friends to uncover using the letter-number key code provided above. In a classroom setting, you may want them to work in groups to brainstorm the camping messages they create for other groups.

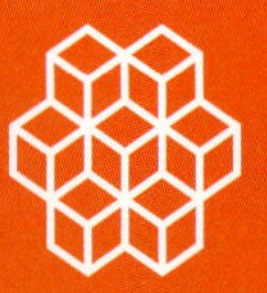

Building Blocks for Creativity

- Reading Skills
- Puzzle Solving Skills

3) Ants, Bears & Corn on the Cob

Camping involves lots of sights, sounds and special gear. Read the list of camping words with the children, and then have them place the words in alphabetical order.

Camping Words

canoeing	sunscreen
blanket	roasting marshmallows
sleeping bag	bird watching
hiking	bug hunts
campfire building	fishing
cooking	hat
swimming	flashlight
ghost stories	insect repellent/bug spray
pitching tents	pillow
tent	guitar
bears	

Challenge

Ask each child to draw a picture that includes as many as possible of the items found in the word list. Then have a parent, teacher or friend see if they can identify the items that are included in the child's picture.

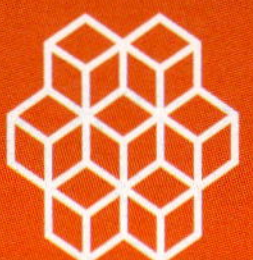

Building Blocks for Creativity

- List Making Skills
- Artistic Skills

4

Rockin' Campfire

Below you will find instructions for adventurous children to create their very own campfire to enjoy all-year-round, using an aluminum pie plate, some soil, stones, popsicle sticks, red/yellow tissue paper and school glue.

Note The aluminum pie plate prevents soil from seeping out.

Rockin' Campfires

Transform an aluminum pie plate into a fabulous miniature campfire!

You will need:

aluminum pie plate

12 to 14 stones per campfire (each about the size of a quarter)

sticks; Note: If you do not have access to outdoor twigs and sticks, popsicle sticks can be substituted.

a handful of soil, dirt or sand for each campfire

white craft/school glue

small scraps of red, orange and yellow tissue paper

a glue gun with glue sticks

Steps:

1. Cover base of an aluminum pie plate with glue, using a paintbrush or your finger to spread the glue out for an even coat.

2. Cover the glued area with dirt or sand and tap off excess. Use your finger to push back a little of the dirt from the edges, all the way around the pie plate, to make room for the stones.

3. Squeeze out a generous amount of white glue around the edge of the base of the pie plate. Press a stone into the glue. Repeat until entire edge of the plate base is covered with stones.

4. If necessary, break sticks into approximately 4 inch pieces. Using white craft clue, build a "fire" with the sticks by positioning the sticks into a teepee formation, gluing as you go. Let everything dry for 2 hours (will not be completely dry, but won't slide around). Another option is for an adult to use a glue gun to glue the bottoms of the sticks to the plate and the tops of the sticks together.

5. Tear tissue paper into small pieces, approximately 1" or 2" squares.

6. Dab several pieces of red tissue paper with glue and position at the top of the campfire. Repeat the dabbing with the orange tissue paper, and lastly with a piece of yellow tissue at the top of the mount.

7. Let project dry completely overnight.

Note A glue gun used can shorten the time needed for each stage of the activity to be completed, but it should be only used by an adult for safety reasons.

Building Blocks for Creativity   • Design Skills

5) Building A Dream Catcher

Dream catchers originated among the Ojibwa nation and have been adopted by a number of different Native American nations. They are believed to help children have good dreams by catching the bad dreams in their nets.

Sleeping outdoors can be intimidating to children, but the dream catchers may improve their chances of having a sound sleep in the Native American tradition.

Wool is woven through the holes punched around the circumference of a paper plate. Beads and feathers are attached and the dream catcher is hung above the child's bed. Children can create their own dream catchers following the instructions below.

Dream Catcher Instructions

You will need:

paper plates (white or coloured)
scissors
hole puncher
markers or crayons

wool or yarn (any colour)
craft beads
craft feathers

Steps:

1. Begin by cutting out the centre of the paper plate (discard the centre). Leave a rim of 2 inches all around the paper plate.

2. Using your hole puncher, punch 8 evenly spaced holes in the rim of the paper plate.

3. Take your markers or crayons and decorate the rim of the paper plate.

4. Measure out your wool 5-6 ft long. Tie one end of the wool to any one of the holes on the rim of the paper plate.

5. Weave the wool across the centre of the plate through a hole. Continue by going back and forth, across the centre to each of the holes. Add the craft beads while weaving the wool from hole to hole. Make sure to loop through each of the holes at least once.

6. As you approach the end of the wool, tie a knot around one of the holes to prevent it from unravelling.

7. Punch 3 additional holes in the dream catcher, near the bottom (bottom and top are at your discretion).

8. Cut 3 more pieces of wool (about 5 inches long each) and tie each one to one of the new holes at the bottom.

9. Select a variety of beads to thread onto each of the 3 wool pieces. Using tape, secure the feather to the end of each piece of wool to prevent the beads from falling off.

10. Cut one last piece of wool (about 5 inches long) and punch a hole at the top of your dream catcher.

11. Thread the wool through the hole and tie a knot. The other end of the wool can be used for hanging your dream catcher in a spot where sweet dreams are welcome!

6) Cooking in a Flash

Camping involves cooking and tasting foods in the great outdoors. The next two recipes are meant to show children how easy it can be to prepare a tasty meal both indoors and outdoors and to help clean up afterwards. They are easy campfire favourites that children can help prepare and then eat together with you.

I'm in the Outdoor Calzone

This next campfire calzone recipe involves pizza dough being flattened and filled with pizza sauce, cheese and a variety of vegetables. Whether it is baked outdoors or indoors, over a fire or in an oven, calzones are a real favourite of campers young and old.

Campfire Calzone

You will need:

1 lb pizza dough (whole wheat is preferable)

1 cup pizza sauce

variety of fillings, to include: sliced olives, chopped tomatoes and onions, sliced green or red peppers, spinach, pineapple, feta cheese, chopped broccoli, diced cooked chicken or sliced mushrooms

2-3 cups shredded cheese

Steps:

1. Spray a baking sheet with non-stick spray and preheat oven to 425°F (convection).

2. Separate dough into 4 portions and on a well-floured surface roll the dough out into a rectangular shape.

3. Spread sauce in the middle and add the desired toppings.

4. Top with shredded cheese, bring the sides of the dough together and press the seams closed all around.

5. Roll the calzone until the seam is facing downwards and brush with olive oil. (At this point, you may choose to sprinkle kosher salt, poppy seeds or sesame seed on top.)

6. Bake on the middle rack for 25-30 minutes, or until the top is a golden brown.

Makes 4 campfire calzones

I'd like S'more please!

S'mores

You will need:

large marshmallows

chocolate chips or broken chunks of your favourite chocolate bar

graham crackers

Steps:

1. Preheat oven to 350°F and spray 9" x 9" squares of aluminum foil with non-stick spray.

2. 1st layer: graham crackers.

3. 2nd layer: marshmallows.

4. 3rd layer: chocolate chips/chunks.

5. Optional layer: graham crackers on top.

6. Fold the aluminum foil and seal the edges.

7. Bake for 7-10 minutes, remove and enjoy!

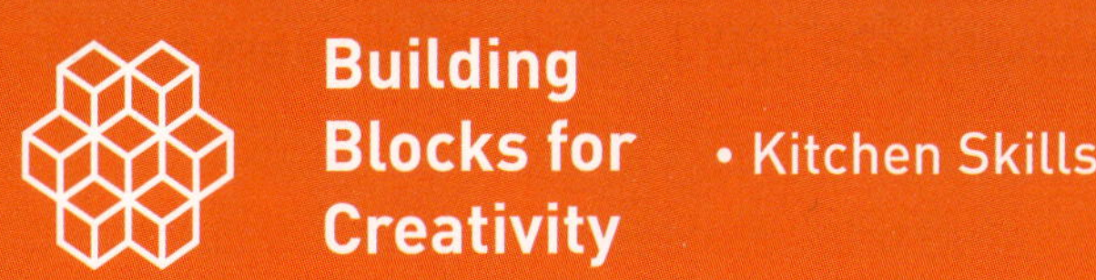

7) Every**birdy** Join In

Encourage children to explore the natural world in their neighbourhood by putting on their scientists caps and looking for birds.

Setting the Seen

Prior to beginning their bird watching adventure, each child can have fun making their own binoculars (using paper towel or toilet paper rolls).

Instructions for Making Binoculars

You will need:

two paper rolls per child
tape or glue
wool or string

Steps:

1. Attach two paper rolls together using glue or tape.

2. Cut a piece of string or wool and attach each end of the string to one of the paper rolls, to hang it around your neck. Note: Make sure the string is cut long enough (approximately 25"-30"), so the binoculars hang loosely around the neck.

Winging It

Next, each child should have a sketch pad and pencil, or camera to record the birds they see in a nearby wooded area, garden or park.

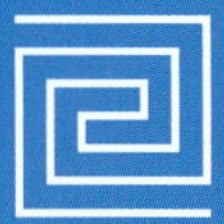

Challenge Have children try to identify the birds seen by comparing the sketches or photographs to illustrations found in books or on the Internet.

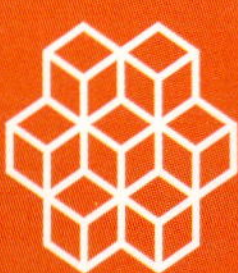

Building Blocks for Creativity
• Observation Skills
• Research Skills

8) **What's Outside My Tent?**

Play *What's Outside My Tent* with your child. This activity explores the different animals and other sounds that you may encounter while camping. In a classroom setting, you can divide the students into pairs to enjoy this game.

One person closes their eyes, while the other(s) makes a camping sound for him or her to identify. The sound maker and guesser can take turns in their roles.

The list of possible sounds below can be given to a child or you can encourage him or her to create their own.

Examples of Sounds Outside The Tent

Growling (bears), whooshing (wind), chirping (crickets), hooting (owls), rushing (water), rustling (leaves), howling (wolves), buzzing (bees)

Challenge ONE   Mime is role playing or acting without sound.

Have each child mime a variety of camping experiences as you call them out verbally either from the list below or as created by you. For example, call out, 'you are cooling beans over a campfire; let's see your preparations and feel the heat of the fire.' This activity takes role playing to the next level by adding movement.

List of Camping Experiences

You are hiking up a big hill

You are walking through tall grass

You are waving away bugs

You are quietly watching a deer

You are fishing in a stream

You are unrolling a sleeping bag

You are getting into a canoe or kayak and paddling

Challenge TWO

Encourage children to use pillows, blankets and chairs, to safely create their own tent.

Suggestions for creating an indoor or outdoor tent together

Indoors:

1. Collect and unfold some sheets and blankets.

2. Grab two to four chairs (at home, sturdy kitchen or dining room chairs work best) and drape the sheets over the chairs.

3. Use a few heavy books (text books and dictionaries work well) to hold the blankets in place. Don't forget to make a doorway!

4. Put together some comfortable things that will make your camping experience more enjoyable such as pillows, sleeping bags, snacks, books, stuffed animals and a flashlight.

5. Now you can turn the light off in the room, put on your flashlight and pretend to be out under the stars!

Outdoors:

Use a blanket for the ground, and a tarp to cover a patio or outdoor table.

Building Blocks for Creativity

- Improvisation Skills
- Listening Skills

9) Science Rubs Me the Right Way

Young learners can examine the textures of the natural world around them by holding paper up against a variety of different textures outdoors, such as bark, and then rubbing different coloured crayons against the paper.

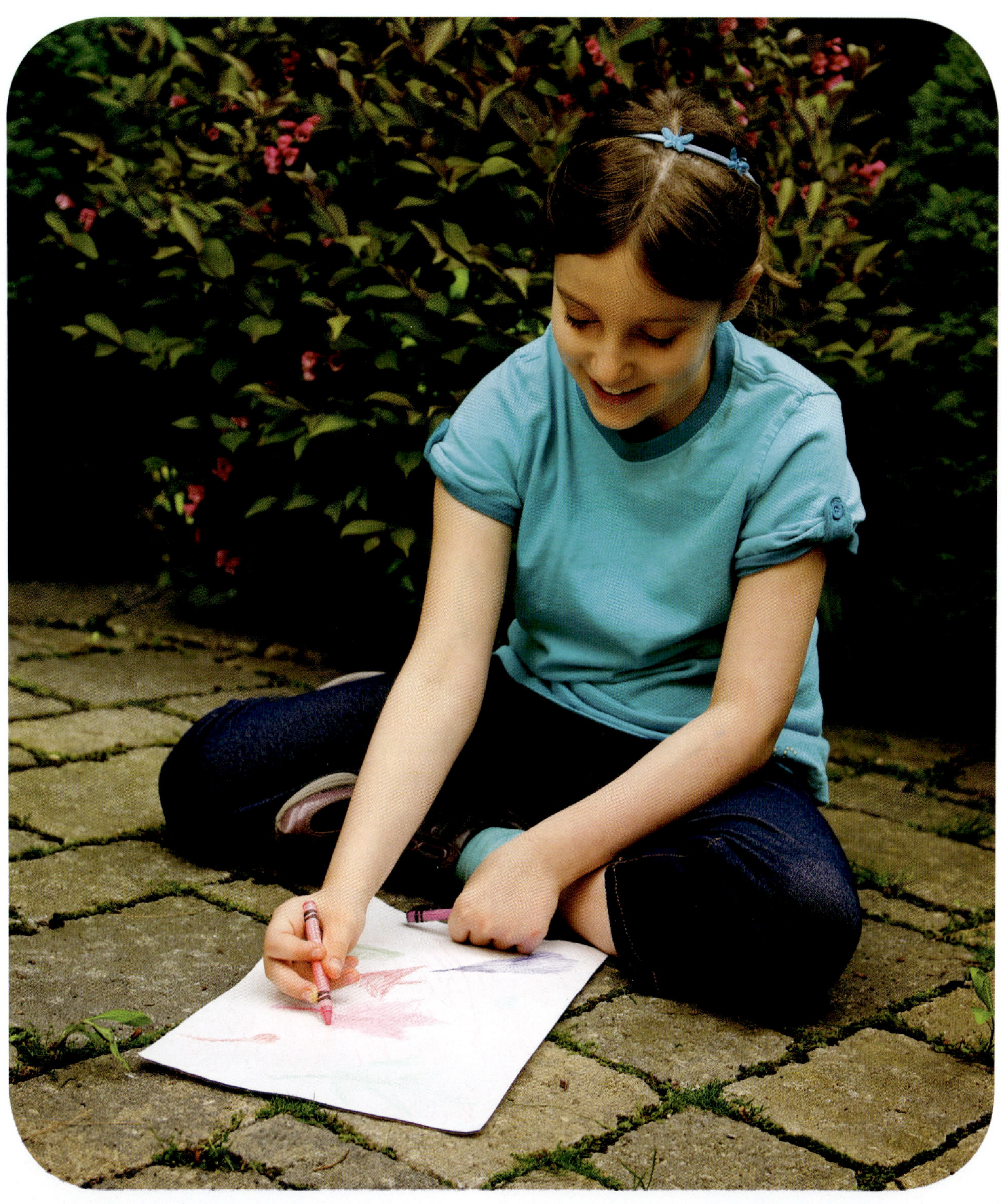

Either go on a walk with children, providing each learner with a piece of paper and crayon to experience natural textures by rubbing crayons against them; or bring 'natural items' such as sticks, leaves, bark, pine needles and petals inside for children to rub with crayons. Have children label the items as they complete each rubbing, so that they can properly identify and compare them in the classroom or at home.

Challenge Ask each child to research plants that should be avoided when camping, e.g., poison ivy or poison oak, and design a warning poster with drawings of the plants.

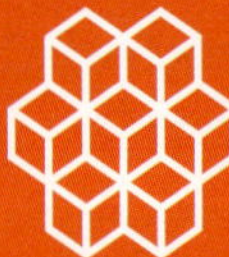

Building Blocks for Creativity
- Recording Skills
- Science Skills
- Artistic Skills

10) Camp Me In

Children now will have their turn to grab some sleeping bags, a tent, other camping accessories and have a *mock* "camp-out" in the school yard or in their back yard. In case of bad weather, move the tent(s) indoors!

Use the crafts already made to create a camping environment. Hang up the rubbings, sketches or photos, any posters and dream catchers that were made.

Create animal noises to make the campout seem real.

Make camping foods and enjoy the great outdoors (or indoors) together.

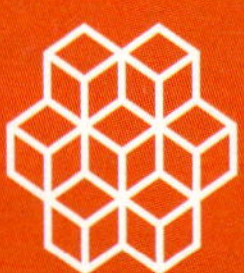

Building Blocks for Creativity
- Planning Skills
- Implementation Skills
- Interpersonal Skills

Appendix A

Scientist's Name: ____

Problem: [Insert the problem your child is trying to solve]

____

____

Hypothesis: [Insert your child's expectation of what the outcome will be]

____

____

____

Materials: [Insert the materials that will be required]

____

____

____

Methods: [Insert the process for completing the experiment]

____

____

____

____

Observations: [Insert what you observed, and where appropriate, draw what you saw]

____

____

____

Conclusions: [Insert your findings based on the results of the experiment]

____

____

Skills Index

1. Creative Problem Solving

Analytical Skills Development of critical thinking skills to analyze ideas, theories and problems.

- Treasured Chocolate **(PAGE 6)**
- Multiply the Fun **(PAGE 45)**
- Do you Feel Fruity? **(PAGE 122)**
- Olive to Play Guessing Game **(PAGE 123)**
- Canoe Guess the Food? **(PAGE 137)**

Brainstorming Skills Ability to come up with ideas to solve problems.

- I Am Sweet **(PAGE 7)**
- Cool Hotel **(PAGE 35)**
- Hibernation is a Sleepy Place **(PAGE 36)**
- Tell Me Just One More Colour **(PAGE 75)**
- You Can Count On Me **(PAGE 40)**
- Cooking with Colour **(PAGE 72)**
- Re-Harmonize **(PAGE 104)**
- Re-Gift **(PAGE 105)**
- Fruit Apeels in Many Ways **(PAGE 132)**

Categorization Skills Ability to group objects and ideas into categories.

- Chocolate Word Search **(PAGE 9)**
- That is Puzzling! **(PAGE 57)**
- Who Really Bugs Me **(PAGE 109)**
- I See Colours **(PAGE 66)**
- Where's De-sign for My Bedroom? **(PAGE 68)**

Comparison Skills Ability to compare objects, ideas and results.

- Chocolate Word Search **(PAGE 9)**
- Paint by Number **(PAGE 38)**
- Unit to Measure it **(PAGE 40)**
- Flag it Down **(PAGE 50)**
- I Feel Blue **(PAGE 79)**
- In sections of the Park I Go **(PAGE 113)**
- Er (Air), Why Does Fruit Brown? **(PAGE 134)**

2. Visualization

Art Appreciation Skills Ability to form opinions about art.

- Chocolate Sculpting **(PAGE 11)**
- Pop Goes the Colours **(PAGE 69)**

Artistic Skills Development of artistic expression.

- Chocolate Sculpting **(PAGE 11)**
- Snowflake... You're Truly Unique! **(PAGE 29)**
- Flag it Down **(PAGE 50)**
- Shake it Baby! **(PAGE 52)**
- Pop Goes the Colours **(PAGE 69)**
- Tell Me Just One More Colour **(PAGE 75)**
- Somewhere over the Rainbow **(PAGE 77)**
- I Dream of Beaches **(PAGE 82)**
- There's Something Fishy About this Activity **(PAGE 91)**
- Leis Time at the Beach (but no Laziness) **(PAGE 86)**
- Fly me to Your Paints **(PAGE 117)**
- Fly Me Away **(PAGE 117)**
- Dragon Fruit Super Heroes (and More) **(PAGE 125)**
- Ants, Bears and Corn on the Cob **(PAGE 139)**
- Building a Dream Catcher **(PAGE 142)**
- Science Rubs Me the Right Way **(PAGE 149)**

Design Skills Ability to create artwork, an object or plan.

- Igloo Sugar Cubes **(PAGE 26)**
- Cool Hotel **(PAGE 35)**
- Patterning a Friendship Bracelet **(PAGE 41)**
- Bean There Done That **(PAGE 58)**
- Piñata Power **(PAGE 54)**
- Where's De-sign for My Bedroom **(PAGE 68)**
- I Dream of Beaches **(PAGE 82)**
- This Sandcastle Puzzles Me **(PAGE 89)**
- Re-Design **(PAGE 99)**
- Re-Create **(PAGE 103)**
- Be a Spider Designer **(PAGE 119)**
- Spicing Things Up **(PAGE 131)**
- Rockin' Campfire **(PAGE 140)**

3. Independent Thinking

Planning Skills Ability to create goals and plans.

Decision Making Skills Ability to choose between different courses of action.

Reading Skills Aimed at improving reading skills for enjoyment and to acquire knowledge.

4. Achieving Original Results

Implementation Skills Ability to plan and execute an idea.

Creative Writing Skills Ability to write fiction, non-fiction and poetry.

5. Communication Skills

Improvisation Skills Ability to act and communication spontaneously.

- Introducing Meteorology **(PAGE 23)**
- Order Anything You Want in my Restaurant **(PAGE 42)**
- On the Ball **(PAGE 55)**
- Somewhere over the Rainbow **(PAGE 77)**
- Re-Invent **(PAGE 102)**
- Flight of the Bumblebee **(PAGE 120)**
- The Very Hungry Me **(PAGE 110)**
- Dragon Fruit Super Heroes (and More) **(PAGE 125)**
- What's Outside My Tent? **(PAGE 147)**

Interpersonal Skills Ability to interact with other people and respond appropriately in social situations.

- Roses are Red, Violets are Blue,
  I'm Writing the Poem You Asked Me To **(PAGE 76)**
- Can You Run Berry Fast? **(PAGE 127)**
- Camp me in **(PAGE 150)**

Interviewing Skills Ability to ask effective questions to obtain information.

- I Spy with My Brown, Blue or Green Eye **(PAGE 78)**
- I Feel Blue **(PAGE 79)**
- Re-Write **(PAGE 106)**

Presentation Skills Ability to communicate ideas to an audience.

- Wrap it Up **(PAGE 21)**
- Introducing Meteorology **(PAGE 23)**

Verbal Skills Ability to express ideas clearly.

- That is Puzzling **(PAGE 57)**
- You Can Count on Me **(PAGE 40)**
- Tell Me Just One more Colour **(PAGE 75)**
- Re-Organize **(PAGE 100)**
- Let's Get Buggy **(PAGE 166)**

6. Relating to Different People and Different Ideas

Language Skills Ability to use appropriate grammar and vocabulary and appreciate different languages.

- Sweet Chocolate Words **(PAGE 8)**
- You Can Count on Me **(PAGE 40)**
- Move and Groove **(PAGE 51)**

Listening Skills Ability to be an effective listener.

- What's Outside my Tent? **(PAGE 147)**

Understanding of Cultural Diversity Openness and ability to learn about different cultures and societies.

- Building a Dream Catcher **(PAGE 142)**